The Folding Screen

The Folding Screen

Charles Hemming with Mark Aldbrook

Rizzoli
NEW YORK

First published in the United States of America in 1999 by
Rizzoli International Publications, Inc.
300 Park Avenue South
New York, NY 10010

First published in the UK in 1999 by
Lund Humphries Publishers Ltd
Park House
1 Russell Gardens
London NW11 9NN

The Folding Screen © 1999 Charles Hemming and Mark Aldbrook

ISBN 0 8478 2179 X

LC 99-70588

Designed by Chrissie Charlton
Typeset by Tom Knott
Printed in Hong Kong by Midas Printing Ltd

Contents

Acknowledgements   page 6

Foreword by Gavin Stamp   7

Introduction   9

The Oriental Screen   10

The Rise of the European Screen   24

The Screen's Revival   50

'Screenness' – The Stage and Film   88

Innovation and Restoration: The Contemporary Screen   94

Glossary   143

Index   144

Acknowledgements

The authors and publishers wish to thank all the artists and galleries who have generously given permission to reproduce works or have provided photographs. Particular thanks go to:

Kenneth Armitage
Stella Beddoe at the Brighton Museum and Art Gallery
Jill Bloomer at Cooper-Hewitt National Design Museum
Janet Carter at Waddesdon Manor
Christopher Wood Gallery
John Cutler
Jim Dine
Martin Durrant at the Victoria & Albert Picture Library
Miwako Eto
Paula Hunt at Mallet & Son (Antiques) Ltd
JAM
Simon Jervis and all at The National Trust
Allen Jones
Richard Kingsett at Messrs Agnews
Francis Kyle
The Mucha Foundation
New Designers in Business
Michael Pick at Stair & Company
Elfreda Powell
Denise Pulford at the Hunterian Museum and Art Gallery
Professor Andrew Sanders
Peyton Skipworth at The Fine Art Society
Gavin Stamp
Messrs Waterhouse and Dodd
Gareth Williams at the Victoria & Albert Museum

Personal thanks are due to Robert Drake and Mark Brittle

Every effort has been made to trace the copyright holders of works and images. We apologise if any institutions or individuals have been incorrectly credited, or if there are any omissions, and would be glad to be notified so that the necessary corrections can be made in any reprint.

Foreword

We have a four-panel folding screen of timber, made I suppose, early this century, into which canvas panels have been inserted. These have been painted to illustrate a pastoral landscape: it is an evocation of the past, running across the whole width of the screen, showing an Elizabethan house and its gardens seen from above, rather in the manner of a seventeenth-century print by Kip. This charming scene was painted for us by Charles Hemming, the talented author of this book.

Until I read his text, I had no idea that the history of the folding screen was so rich and so interesting. I knew that a screen could be at once functional and a decorative object, and that – in Japan at least – it could also be architecture. Now I learn that architects like Norman Shaw's partner, William Eden Nesfield, and the Art Nouveau designer, Henri van der Velde, occasionally designed screens. And, of course, Charles Hemming is not the only painter to turn his attention to decorating them: there are screens painted by Cézanne and by Whistler and by many other famous names – many of them illustrated here. Once I found it amusing that, in *Brideshead Revisited* by Evelyn Waugh, Charles Ryder turned his screen, painted by Roger Fry, to the wall once he thought he had become more sophisticated; now I should rather like to rescue it from that cupboard full of buckets and mops where it had been exiled.

I like the fact that screens need not be for anything but can just stand there, looking beautiful. In modern times – since the advent of central heating – perhaps their main function in both farces and films has been to encourage modesty by shielding women undressing, and so enabling discarded underwear suddenly to appear over the top. Now I learn that the erotic potential of the screen informed Marcel Duchamp when he painted *The Bride Stripped Bare by her Bachelors* on glass panels, making it an inverted metaphor of its intended purpose.

As an artist himself, Mr Hemming brings the story right up to date by including the work of modern artists who have wittily exploited the nature of the screen as an art object. Now that he has given us this splendid account of the folding screen, past and present, perhaps he should return to decorating them again. I imagine a neo-Surrealist screen, perhaps covered in stuck-on labels and newspaper cuttings, with a *trompe l'œil* depiction of a slip, nylons and a brassière hanging down in front of it. Charles Hemming could certainly paint such a thing convincingly.

Gavin Stamp

Introduction

'The Chinaman in the screen' is a colloquialism born out of the origins of the folding screen, which came originally to Europe from Ming dynasty China. In the West, the style and content of the screen reflected the changes in European society and culture between the Renaissance and the French Revolution. Its arrival in Europe resulted from rapidly expanding exploration and trade; its development, the assimilation of those features of the Far East which the West found stimulating and rewarding. In the eighteenth century – a high point in its popularity and variety – the screen mirrored the wealthy minority's image of its own immediate society and what it chose to see of the world beyond, even in terms of satire and mockery. The screen recorded images of other cultures and continents, and in the theatre it acted as a symbol of the façades of the Age of Reason.

In its flexibility the folding screen was analogous to the cultural winds which have tugged and twisted the Western world from the French Revolution until the present day. With its aristocratic connotations, it should have been a casualty of the Age of Revolution. It was an image of decorum and of the values of the establishment; but, predictably, rebels seeking to destroy the status quo quickly aped those whose power they had overthrown, and retained the screen in their new regime, decked out with Imperial decorations. Ironically, it was in Britain and most other parts of conservative Western Europe that it suffered injury from a new classical revival in design, and nearly disappeared. Then, with changes in domestic social behaviour, and as a hand-crafted object symbolising a rejection of the crude decorative excesses of mass-machine production, it enjoyed a huge resurgence at the end of the nineteenth century.

During the first decades of the twentieth century, the screen became a symbol of aesthetic elitism and design quality, then of an aggressive modernism, and in the 1960s, largely in the United States, evolved into a contemporary installation art object. Finally, to a generation of people with a high level of visual literacy, it became a custom-built creation which could reflect any period of the past or present, as quality decorative furnishing, painted art object, or sculpture. From the beginning of the nineteenth century until the 1930s, screen development was largely dominated by European design; from the 1930s until the 1980s, by American.

Because of the changing function and nature of screens, it is appropriate to discuss the different kinds and their social history until the middle of the nineteenth century. Thereafter, when the screen, following its revival, became chiefly an exclusive object of craft or artistic experiment, the focus of the text shifts to individual screens of prominence and the artists who created them.

The Oriental Screen

Fig.1
Chinese Coromandel (twelve panels)
*c.*1690
Incised lacquer portraying birds
350 x 540 cm (138 x 212½ in)
Courtesy of Mallett & Son (Antiques) Ltd, London

Screens, *Byōbus*, and Paravents from Coromandel

The *Clove* was the first English ship to return from Japan. She arrived in 1614 via the 'shores of Coromandel', carrying 'Japanese wares ... Trunks, Beoubes, Cupps, dishes of all sorts and of a most excellent varnish'.[1] The 'Beoubes' were *byōbu*s – screens. The Dutch had been shipping them since 1602, and the stream from China and Japan increased when the French emulated the East India Companies of the Dutch and English by founding the *Compagne des Indes* in 1660. By the close of the century, French and British 'Indiamen' were carrying homeward cargoes of between fifty and a hundred packing cases of Chinese screens or 'paravents' at a time.

The Chinese had invented the folding screen, and Chou dynasty poets mention it early in the second century BC. It seems to have been a large, heavy, wood-panelled object hinged with cloth or leather straps, not meant to be moved frequently. Its adornment was considered a fine art, and the decoration that was applied to its panels, which were either lacquered or painted, portrayed all the desirable aspects of life. Subsequently it acquired a border patterned with those delightful articles which one might wish to take to the grave. In the eighth century it reached Japan, together with the technique of lacquering, and until about the beginning of the Ming dynasty (1368) the Chinese considered it an object worthy of their most eminent artists' attentions. From then on its design status in China declined and its embellishment was considered a minor art, the province of skilled artisans who repeated formulae. Not so in Japan.

Although the Japanese venerated Chinese art, from around the tenth century onwards they transformed the folding screen. Their houses lacked the permanent inner walls of the Chinese, and so the salient feature of their *byōbu* was flexibility enhanced by mobility. Although their lacquered screens remained similar to those of the Chinese, their painted counterparts were lighter, generally smaller, and as a result more durable than their Chinese predecessors, and owed their success to their innovative construction. Such screens had a light, precision-made frame of specially prepared, seasoned wood, over which paper was laid in interlocking layers; these layers also overlapped from panel to panel, creating a strong, almost invisible paper hinge. This hinge enabled the artist to view the whole screen as one continuous picture plane, not, as formerly, merely as a series of panels with gaps between them, which forced the artist into an episodic, repetitive, or disjointed design. As a result, the *byōbu* was considered an appropriate paint surface by some of Japan's most eminent artists.

By the time the Europeans arrived in Japan (when two Portuguese sailors landed there by accident in 1545) Japanese and Chinese styles of painting and interior decorative art had been applied simultaneously in Japanese residences. Chinese art had been regarded as special and precious in Japan, and throughout the fifteenth century it had been common practice to hang Chinese scrolls or paper 'wall' pictures on the front of Japanese screens of the Yamato-e (traditional Japanese) style.

1 Hugh Honour, *Chinoiserie*, John Murray, 1961, p.43.

This reveals not only that the two aesthetic traditions interacted, but also that the Japanese themselves viewed the screen as evocative of China.

There were three types of screen in Japan. One was a sliding panel, the *fusuma*: a paper-faced partition, sliding in tracks, which was used to divide interior spaces in *shoin* residences – a style of architecture of the social elite of the Muromachi period (1392-1573), when Japan was dominated by the Ashikaga shoguns of the Muromachi district of Kyoto. The second, the *tsitsuae*, was a stationary single-panel screen used at the house entrance to denote status or a ceremony in progress; and the third was a folding screen, or *byōbu*. This portable, accordion-folding fixture was used both for the division of space and for decoration in traditional Japanese architecture. When the Europeans arrived, the paper-panelled screen existed in two 'styles': the Yamato-e, which had subjects of traditional life and established narrative tales; and the Kanga – 'Chinese pictures' – based on pictorial styles, materials, and subjects recently imported from China. The Kanga style enjoyed the greater prestige within Japan during the trading period with Europe, before traffic was curtailed by the Shogun around 1650. Kanga was the style practised by the Kano school of professional artists who were often painters to the Shogun. As a result, those Japanese painted screens which were either commissioned by the Jesuits or reached Europe were produced by the lesser artists of the Kano school. The finest always remained in Japan. In light of this, and the sheer distances involved, it is scarcely surprising that seventeenth-century Europeans were unclear whether their purchases came from China or Japan.

However, it was not the light Japanese paper screen which arrived in Europe in the early seventeenth century, but the heavy Chinese-style 'Coromandel'. This often exquisitely made type of screen was generally very large, as much as ten feet in height and twenty broad, with twelve panels or 'leaves' of lacquered and gilded wood. Soon afterwards, shipments were supplemented with smaller, five-fold screens, made in the same way.

Lacquer was not unknown in Europe before these screens arrived. It had been used by Venetian artists in the sixteenth century, but had quickly fallen from favour, and had been of a different chemical consistency from that used in the Far East. True Chinese lacquer consisted of resin from the *Rhus vernicifera*, a tree originating in China and later introduced to Japan. Crude lac was a grey fluid which had to be used very quickly, drying and darkening on exposure to air. It was therefore impossible to ship it to Europe raw, where it only appeared as a finished product.

The preparation of boards for the lacquer application was a very lengthy and precise process, and the application of the lacquer highly skilled, labour-intensive and time-consuming. Care was also needed, because raw lac could cause painful skin rashes. The Chinese and Japanese processes varied only slightly. First a thin coat of natural lac was applied to the wood. When this dried, a second coat mixed with fine earth, and at times combined with grasses, was applied to fill any cracks in the wood. A sheet of stretched cloth went over that, to form a uniform surface for all subsequent coats, and to act as a cushion against any jolts which might cause cracking; it also prevented the intrusion of water. This preparation obliterated the texture of the wooden surface. Eight coats of lacquer were then applied, in Japan all including a mixture of very fine earth. Each of these took an average of three days to dry, depending upon the humidity of the air, and each coat was carefully pummiced until it was silky smooth. Then an eleventh coat of pure natural lacquer was given to stabilise the layers beneath. This was followed by six more coats of lacquer and clay. The eighteenth coat was the first one into which any coloured pigment was introduced, and then two more coloured coats were applied, each carefully pummiced. Several more coats could be added after this, including the applied decoration. The Chinese might add less earth in the lower layers.

The application of the decoration was where the greatest differences lay. On Chinese Coromandel screens the decoration was incised. This meant scratching a design on the surface, cutting it into the lacquer with a very sharp knife, and then filling the resulting groove with gesso and coloured pigment, or gesso and gilt. The liquid lacquer itself had often been tinted with powdered pigment on application, the most common 'ground' colour (that is, the predominant background tone of the screen) being black; vermilion was the next most popular, then a greeny-brown called *tête de nègre* by Europeans, and aubergine. Writing in the nineteenth century the French antiquary and connoisseur Albert Jacquemart considered it was the Japanese who had developed the vermilion (scarlet) lacquer, and by the seventeenth century the Japanese and Chinese courts were exchanging work whose techniques were cross-fertilised. These materials were often augmented with ivory inlay or mother-of-pearl, or appliqués of agate, crystal, lapis lazuli, coral or jade.

The Japanese were familiar with the Chinese Coromandel technique, but rarely used it for their lacquer work. Instead, they usually decorated the surface of the lacquer, using a built-up gesso called gofun. This relief-pattern gesso was generally painted gold, while gold dust was frequently sprinkled over the surface before the application of the final lacquer coat.

The very term Coromandel reflected the romantic vagueness and geographical confusion of the Far East in the European mind. Coromandel is a portion of the east Indian coast near Madras, and had nothing to do with the production of lacquered screens other than being a transferring point for Far Eastern goods being shipped to Europe by England's East India Company. The English found this necessary as the aggressive and powerful Dutch fleet forced them to make a detour on their homeward run. Of course, more confusingly, goods from Japan passed through Coromandel, being referred to interchangeably as

Fig.2
Chinese Coromandel (twelve panels)
c.1663.
Incised lacquer
196 x 525 cm (77 x 207 in)
Courtesy of *The Connoisseur* Magazine
(John Leander Esq.)

'India', 'Japan' and 'China' wares, while the term 'japanned' came to refer to any high-gloss lacquered finish. Seventeenth-century inventories use these terms so indiscriminately that it is impossible to identify the true origins of many objects which they describe.

Chinese Coromandels almost always had a wide border around the main design, often featuring utensils, flowers, calligraphy and animals. The origins of such motifs were the 'Hundred Objects' needed by the screen's owner in the afterlife. A twelve-fold Chinese Coromandel lacquered screen of about 1690, showing fabulous birds in an exquisite woodland, the leaves and feathers incised in gold leaf on black lacquer counterpointed with blue-grey and scarlet lacquer, is typical of a high-quality Coromandel screen (fig.1). The wide border showing vases, urns, miniature temples and bouquets would convey nothing but exotic decoration to the European aristocrat, but in China symbolised these things being retained after death; naturally, then, the one image that never occurs in the borders is a human being. Another twelve-panel screen (fig.2) of 1663, seventeen feet wide by seven high, displays a garden and lake with green incised lacquer portraying rocky outcrops; blossoms and the robes of figures strolling and boating in the landscape are white, silver and iridescent pink. As was typical, water is rendered by rhythmic incisions resembling shining hair, while the whole has a broad border containing vases, flowers and eating utensils. These design conventions continued when screens were made for export. A fine Chinese lacquer screen of about 1720 (fig.3) shows a similar scene with figures holding kites and standards, while the lower border shows fantastic animals of many kinds. The verso (back) of the screen bears calligraphy, generally unreadable by the European buyer. Even when the design of the main area might be influenced by or even incorporate scenes from Europe, which the Chinese artists copied from engravings, the funerary border remained. This cross-fertilisation became more common as the seventeenth century closed and the demand for lacquer screens of great size became insatiable.

In the big draughty manor houses of England and the spacious *châteaux* of France, these screens were not only visually impressive but also functional. Provided the owner had the manpower to move them, some also travelled. For his success at Blenheim in 1704, the Duke of Marlborough was presented by the Holy Roman Emperor with a superb Chinese Coromandel, which had been commissioned by the Jesuits as one of a pair for Leopold I on his becoming Emperor in 1658. Marlborough took the screen with him on his subsequent campaigns, probably forming a background to his headquarters at Ramillies (1706) and Malplaquet (1709).

By the time Marlborough was presented with his screen, imports into Western Europe of lacquered goods of all kinds, not just screens, had caused an economic crisis amongst British and French craftsmen. Their work was of as high a standard as anything from abroad and their joinery frequently superior, but they could not produce lacquer. While

English joiners had finally petitioned Parliament for a halt to these imports, the French – who had been inserting into their rococo work lacquered boards either cut from screens or specifically commissioned in China and Japan – set out to develop a lacquered product of their own, based on a native substitute for the *Rhus vernicifera* (which could not be transplanted into Europe).

The pre-lacquering process itself was first fully described in Europe in a treatise by George Parker and John Stalker, published in England in 1688, but the first scientific analysis of Chinese lacquer was carried out by an Italian Jesuit, Filippo Bonanni, who published his results in 1720, and then a Frenchman, Antoni d'Emery, developed the first recipe for the European substitute. The advantage of d'Emery's lacquer – born of the necessity of being made from a different chemical composition – was that it did not take as long as the Chinese substance to dry and polish. Because it was a speedier process, this lacquer was frequently applied with less care than the Chinese, but it was highly effective, and became popular in time to save the livelihoods of many craftsmen.

From the last decade of the seventeenth century until well into the eighteenth, British and French craftsmen produced screens in the Chinese style. By the mid-eighteenth century the alternative, smaller, five-fold screens from China had begun to reduce or dispense with the border, sometimes retaining it only at the top and bottom in the manner of a frieze and a very low dado or skirting board, while the content of the border had become 'secular', consisting of landscapes or flowers. At times these smaller screens were borderless, in the manner of the scarlet and gold four-panel lacquer screen illustrated (fig. 5).

However, it was the perspectiveless style of the Chinese and Japanese artwork which made one of the most forceful impressions on European makers. To the Europeans, the visual language was unfamiliar, and although the screen border patterns joined, the central designs often appeared to them to be disjointed. It is even possible that unassembled screens arriving in cases may have been reassembled out of sequence. Thus, European imitators making their own panels, mimicking the Chinese style, deliberately made them disjointed. In these reproductions, a wall or bridge disappears abruptly at a panel hinge, and a bird or hill begins. It appears that depictions of walls in the originals were often misunderstood and seen merely as bands of pattern when these lacquered screens were either copied or assembled. The effect of this 'stringing together' of patterns reinforced the perception amongst many artists that the screen was essentially an object produced in a certain style via specific techniques, rather than a serious aesthetic achievement.

By the late eighteenth century the big Chinese screens which retained their borders had resolved them almost solidly into close-packed patterns of flowers and leaves (fig. 7). It was this configuration which continued into the 1860s. During the eighteenth century the town of Ning-po became the centre of 'cabinet work', remaining so until it was

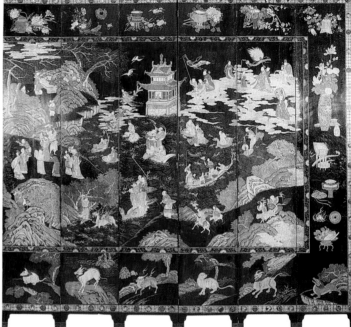

Fig.3
Chinese screen (twelve panels)
c.1720
Incised lacquer with calligraphy on reverse
108 x 600 cm (42.5 x 236 in)
Courtesy of Mallett & Son (Antiques) Ltd, London

destroyed in the 1860s during the Tai-ping rebellion, and many of these screens were made there. An observer remarked that:

'Round and rectangular footstools, tables and *étagères* complete this style of furniture, with large screens and picture frames enclosing sentences or emblems, often in relief, on a lacquered ground.

'The last pieces we have mentioned are generally in red or black wood, and of very hard quality. The ... folding screens ... in a word the ordinary manufactures of Ning-po, are in yellow wood encrusted with ivory, or in brown decorative wood encrusted with yellow pako.'[2]

While Chinese screens were becoming a relatively standardised, commercially produced item of trade, French lacquer screens were being produced to an exceptionally high standard. The craft was centred in Paris, where its most famous master, Robert Martin, held a japanning patent for his technique called *vernis martin*, a relief lacquering 'in the style of Japan and China'.[3] Under royal patronage, Martin enjoyed enormous prestige, and according to Voltaire the quality of his lacquer work surpassed that of the Chinese.[4]

2 Albert Jacquemart, *A History of Furniture*, Chapman & Hall, 1874.
3 Janet Adams, *The Decorative Folding Screen*, Thames and Hudson, 1982, p.60.
4 Adolf Reichwein, *China and Europe*, Routledge, 1996, p.35; and Janet Adams, op.cit. p.61.

Fig.4
Japanese screen (six panels)
c.1720
Painted flowers on gold leaf on paper
180 x 450 cm (71 x 177 in)
Courtesy of Mallett & Son (Antiques) Ltd,
London

Fig.6
Chinese screen (five panels)
*c.*1750
Incised lacquer
255 x 250 cm (100½ x 98½ in)
Courtesy of Stair & Company, London

Fig.7
Chinese screen (eight panels)
*c.*1820
Incised gilt black lacquer
206.5 x 432 cm (81½ x 170 in)
Courtesy of Mallett & Son (Antiques) Ltd, London

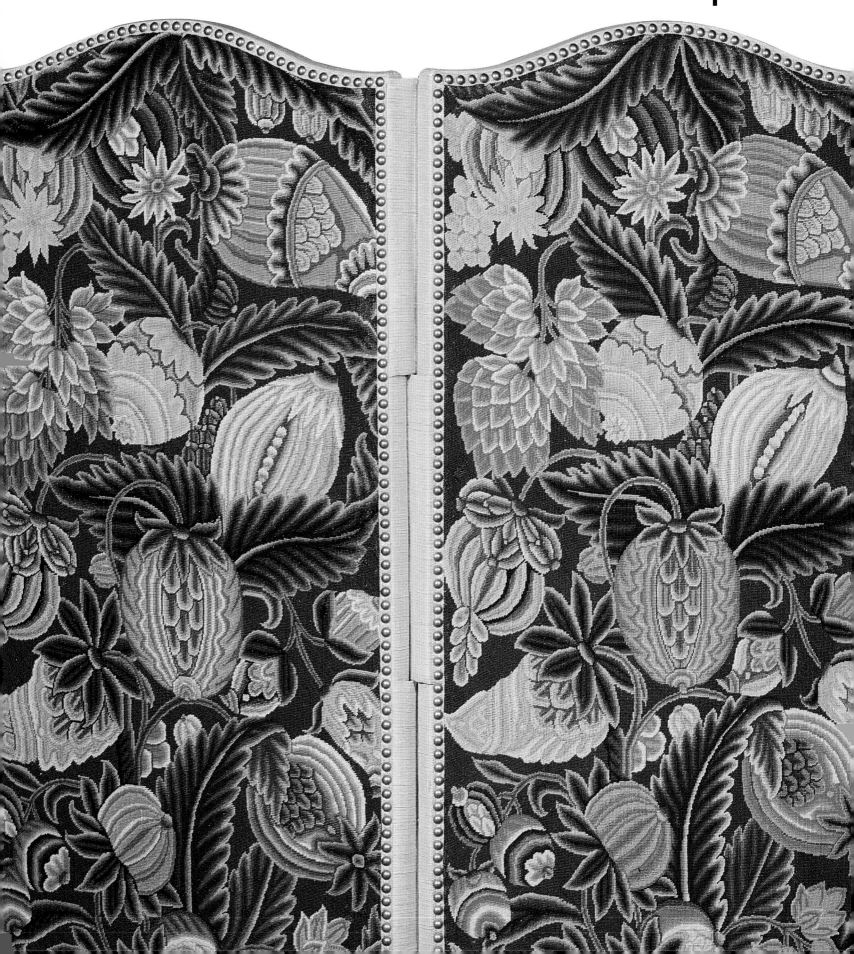

Screen

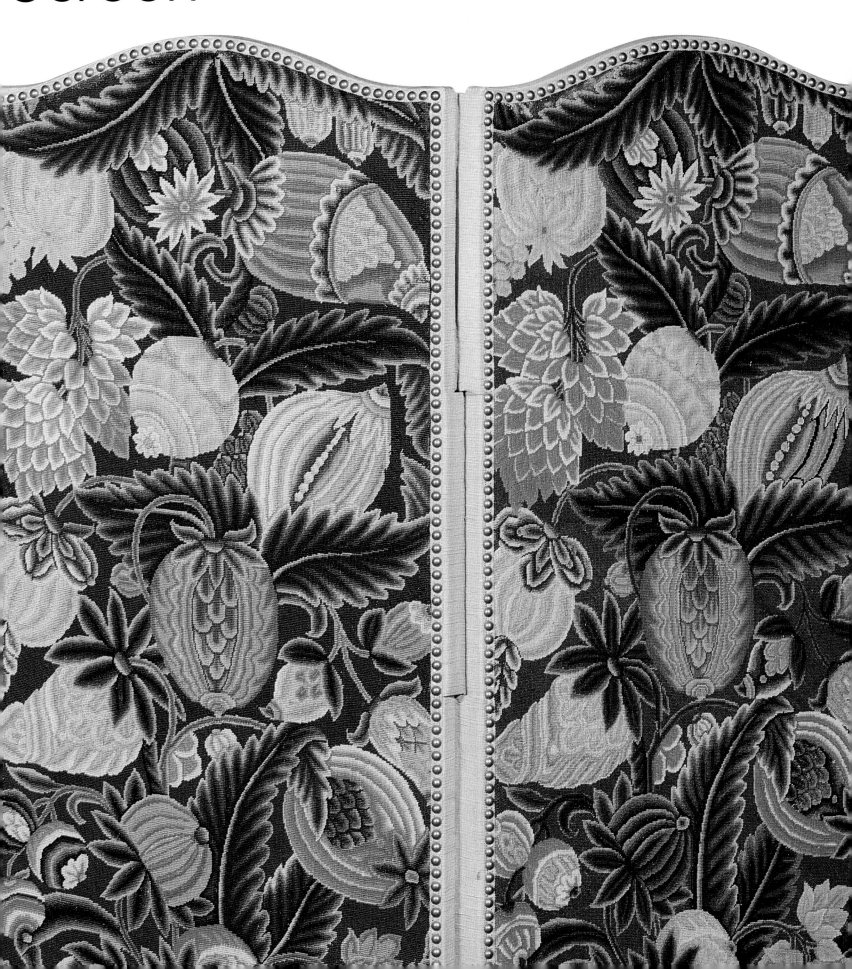

Supple Alternative – The Leather Screen

Fig.8
Spanish Iberian screen (four panels)
Late eighteenth century
Incised leather with *putti* (cherub)
pattern
240 x 240 cm (94½ x 94½ in)
Private Collection

From the fourteenth century leather had been embossed, stamped and painted and used for wall hangings. Usually it was mounted on a wooden frame for this, and painting and gilding the leather normally enhanced the relief patterns of the stamping technique and reflected and increased a room's candle-light.

By the early eighteenth century the numerous leather workers of London and the Netherlands had begun advertising and producing their equivalent of the Coromandel screen with considerable success, and were soon emulated by their counterparts in Spain and Italy. Their product had a number of great advantages for the client. Leather was relatively light, extremely durable, could be cut to any size or shape, and because the screen was produced locally it was much cheaper than an import from thousands of miles away. Better still, the client's own personal taste could be reflected in the product as the craftsman could do exactly as he was bidden, with no cumbersome cultural or geographical intermediary. There was also a very large colour range immediately available.

These handsome screens were generally ordered with four to eight panels rather than the Chinese six or twelve, and were of considerably reduced height compared to the towering Chinese Coromandels. The subjects of these screens varied, but throughout the eighteenth century generally included fruit, flower, scrollwork or bird designs, vignettes with oriental motifs, architectural decorations, or celebrations of events set in a landscape. Typically the surface of the leather was stamped to form a relief pattern, and then highlights were gilded, while other details were painted in oil and then protected with an oil glaze. Occasionally the background of a scene might be gilded and the figures, birds and other creatures painted in contrast. A fine Spanish Cordova leather screen of about 1760 shows an elegant chinoiserie (Chinese-style) pattern over its eight tall and relatively narrow panels, the oriental buildings, walls, and flights of steps forming what is essentially a series of broad zig-zag patterns in red-gold over the blue-black background (fig.9). The lake in the foreground is portrayed by spreads of lily pads resembling big sequins. The overall rhythmic energy of the screen is striking, but its execution is much bolder – heavier – than one might expect from an Oriental maker.

The fact that the material was leather is turned to great advantage by the craftsmen, for the use of pins (coach studs) along the edges of the panels forms a striking pattern, manipulated with great sophistication. The studs are on the front edge of the panel when the hinge opens away from the observer, but they are on the inside edge when it is towards the observer. When on the front edge the studs are framed by contrasting leather. This means that the design is divided by vertical strips which never become too heavy or frequent but are used to frame the design – an aesthetic virtue borne out of necessity. To balance these verticals, there is a horizontal border in Chinese style but heavily framed.

Fig.9
Spanish Cordova screen (eight panels)
c.1760
Incised leather with chinoiserie design
240 x 320 cm (94½ x 126 in)
Courtesy of Mallett & Son (Antiques) Ltd,
London

The 'Western' chinoiserie of the early to mid-eighteenth century screens is very marked, but as the eighteenth century progressed the subjects of leather screens moved away from their original Chinese or Japanese inspiration and bore a closer resemblance to contemporary narrative landscape painting. An Iberian four-fold leather screen of the late eighteenth century (fig.8), for example, shows no trace of chinoiserie. Instead, cherubs occupy the centre of twelve cartouches (decorative panels) embellished with the familiar grapes, cornucopias and roses associated with European rococo and the classical idyll. Neither is there the sense of visual weight that is present in the Cordova screen of some thirty years earlier, and there is a sensuous curvaceousness of touch more redolent today of a bedchamber than a public room.

In England, the leather screen became a medium for hunting and pastoral scenes set on estates, the figures painted in oil on a gilded background. Frequently each of the three or four panels was divided into two or three levels, each showing a different scene or event. These English screens generally had a pronounced element of informality about their subject and composition, and a simplicity of execution which borders on the naïve. Many were made in the client's local region, by people who were primarily craftsmen rather than artists, and in some cases were painted by dilettante of the gentry. As a result they often possessed a freshness, charm and individualism which most of the more elegant, sophisticated Continental screens in leather and tapestry did not display.

Italian artists utilised a vibrant palette, well suited to an Oriental style already assimilated into the Italian decorative aesthetic as a result of the Silk Route, which had placed Italian cities such as Venice at the heart of East-West trade since the fourteenth century. Not surprisingly, therefore, Coromandel lacquer work had been less of a concern to the Italians than their English and French counterparts, and the eighteenth century saw a wide use of leather, silk and wood in their screens. Indeed, as Janet Adams has pointed out, the spread of the screen through Italy in the seventeenth and eighteenth centuries is as much an illustration of fashion as necessity; for the western and southern Italian states were being influenced by the tastes of Spain and France and by northern and eastern Austria.[5]

An Indispensable Object

The fabric screen is thought to have been introduced in France not long after Oriental screens first became available in Europe. Inventories of house contents from the late 1660s list embroidered screens and other cloth screens painted with flowers, wild animals and Chinese subjects.

Throughout the late seventeenth and the whole of the eighteenth century the screen was an ubiquitous part of the French court, and of aristocratic and upper bourgeois life. In the grand *châteaux*, draughty beyond the imagining of the late twentieth century, large screens

5 Janet Adams, op.cit. p.96.

insulated groups at gatherings of all kinds and shielded them from the social intrusion of others, including their armies of servants. Much of the etiquette and intrigue which is the stuff of plays, opera and novels, was not simply aided but was encouraged by the presence of folding screens. Large ones were used in the great public rooms, small, light, mobile ones in bedrooms, and they appear constantly in the background of narrative and genre paintings or 'conversation pieces' of the eighteenth century, where their painted and woven patterns are recorded in great detail. In France the five-foot high, four- to eight-panel fabric screen in a simple lacquered or carved wooden frame was probably the most popular variety, matching the upholstery of the furniture and acting as one with it, perhaps separating a group of musicians from a draught and at the same time separating their audience from the sight of a pile of music scores on a table and an assignation going on beside it.

The absence of a screen could be keenly felt. At Versailles, where Louis XIV carried his obsession for symmetry in garden and building to the point of dogma, a screen was forbidden in case it unbalanced the mathematical precision of a social gathering, prompting Louis' shivering wife to remark that she would 'die of symmetry'.

The screens commissioned by the French royal house were *tours de force* involving many craftsmen and artists – cabinet makers, carvers, gilders and upholsterers – each one usually being the recognised master in his field. The factory at Savonnerie produced superb tapestries for screens, while the Lyons workshops wove silks, these makers supplying the finest tapestry and cloth screens until after the French Revolution. The dominating feature of all these great French screens and countless smaller ones was their sumptuousness and symmetry.

At the end of the seventeenth century English woven screens were often of very high quality, but moderate in size, and possessed a general looseness of design which reflected the relative informality of the houses and society which produced them. An English wool and silk screen (fig.10) of a woodland with birds and flowers has a density and visual weight offset by its vigour and great charm. All three panels are self-contained but form a unified motif, naturalistic but without any attempt being made at symmetry within the design.

By contrast, a pair of French *Régence* embroidered screens of around 1730 (fig.11), each approximately the size of the earlier English screen, display the elegance and symmetry which established itself in the eighteenth century as a major character of French design. Although in the early eighteenth century much needlepoint work was quite unaffected, as the century advanced so did the fabric screen in England, reaching technical excellence the equal of anything on the Continent, but remaining looser in design to the end.

By the 1730s French embroidered screens were frequently designed by artists, generally painters, such as Boucher, Lancret, Huet and Watteau,

Fig.10
English tapestry screen (three panels)
Late seventeenth century
Wool and silk on linen canvas mounted
on mahogany frame
145 x 210 cm (57 x 82½ in)
Courtesy of Stair & Company, London

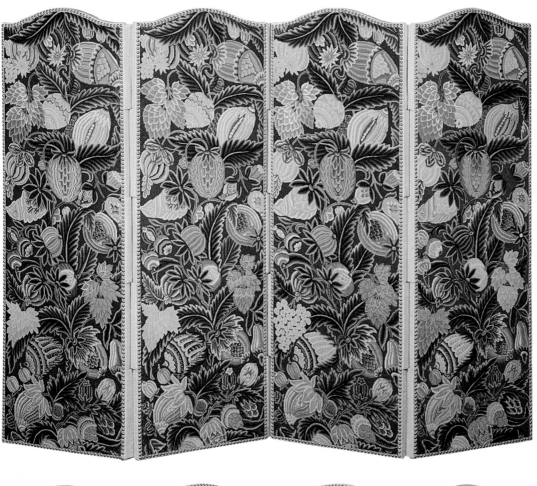

Fig.11
French *Régence* screens (a pair, four panels)
*c.*1730
Needlework
156 x 326 cm (61½ x 128½ in)
Courtesy of Mallett & Son (Antiques) Ltd, London

and were highly elaborate. They no longer depended upon Chinese subjects, although these remained highly popular and very common. Pastoral scenes – *fêtes de campagne* – were great favourites, generally depicting highly langorous shepherds and shepherdesses in arbours and grottos, with cattle, flute players – the god Pan – and musicians beneath spreading trees, all the idyllic paraphernalia associated with Virgil's 'Georgics', which were even more popular (certainly more often read) in England, where Watteau had originally made his name. These idealised groups were usually framed with urns, coils of acanthus, cornucopia, doves, roses, scrolls, ribbons, garlands and cartouches. Architecture featured in these compositions in the form of terraces, statues and pavilions, providing backdrops to aristocratic groups at leisure, but so did wild animals, and the creatures of the forest and hunt. Stags, hounds, swans and storks of the European countryside were augmented by lions, leopards, parrots, macaws, peacocks and long-tailed monkeys. Even serpents appeared amongst the foliage. Such screens varied in size: anything from six to seven feet high and twelve wide with six or seven panels, to five feet high with two or three.

English fabric screens of the seventeenth and eighteenth centuries are far less formal than their French counterparts. Most English owners of high quality screens appear to have selected them as a projection of their own interests and personality. The design and execution of screens by artists working in the style of Lancret and using his compositions indicates no mere accessory; screens deployed in such interiors required the highest quality of decoration from the best possible artists. These artists also designed and executed other areas of the decor of which the screen formed an integral part; but while there is no evidence that Lancret actually painted any folding screens in person, Jacques de Lajoue of his circle carried them out, as did Watteau. It appears that Watteau also painted fans and screens for his friends, usually as gifts, and while none of these are known to have survived, it would seem probable that they were vignettes from his paintings or motifs from the subordinate design details they contained.

Certain subjects were especially suitable for the screen. The four-panel format invited the quartet of the Four Times of Day, usually defined as dawn (or morning), morning (or noon, luncheon), afternoon, and evening (twilight or night), with the social activities associated with those periods portrayed as vignettes on each succeeding panel. An elegant screen adapted from Lancret's *Les Quatre Heures du Jour* (now in the Victoria & Albert Museum, London) is typical, its four panels being respectively *Le Matin*, *Le Midi*, *L'Après-midi*, and *Le Soir* – awakening and bathing, taking coffee, playing board games, and attending a *soirée*. The Four Seasons was another favourite, blending with the hunt, natural or pastoral world decorations of so many *châteaux*, or two or three screens with the theme The Twelve Months of the Year. In the 1890s these subjects were to return in celebrated screens by Alphonse Mucha, one of the leading commercial exponents of Art Nouveau.

Because the Italians had always preferred their screens painted on wood, silk or leather, the finest were inevitably in these media. Although their pallet leant itself to the chinoiserie of pagodas, birds, parasoled figures and exotic dragons, their artists and artisans also worked uninfluenced by the Chinese fashion. One of Italy's greatest wood carvers, Giuseppe Maria Bonzanigo (1744-1820), a Piedmontese who later settled in Turin, was responsible for the exquisite carved frames of a series of screens, the forms of which were repeated on the silk panels, and the oil-painted wooden panels of another screen. The subjects are architectural and mythical, and in no way Chinese.

There was a great diversity of styles among Italian screens, and although many Italian craftsmen worked in the wealthier parts of Europe, those who remained in Italy often had to use less costly materials than those which were available in Britain and France. This was because, despite being exuberant and colourful, eighteenth- and nineteenth-century Italian states were financially poor and politically divided. One creative advantage of this, however, was the lack of such all-powerful trade guilds as existed in Britain which tended to encourage a dominance of certain styles. The Italians also enjoyed the absence of an autocratic court, such as that found in France, which dictated to the socially mobile what they should aspire to and admire.

Italy never succumbed to chinoiserie to anything like the extent of her northern contemporaries, who, anyway, by the mid-eighteenth century were encountering the three-way interplay of style from rococo, Gothic and neo-classical motifs, which gradually ousted anything recognisably Chinese. From the mid-1750s onwards the chinoiserie fashion was even being acerbically mocked by some of its own leading practitioners.

An Elegant Mockery – Singerie

It was the marriage of fine art and the decorative arts in France, through the work of eminent artists such as Huet and Lancret in the eighteenth century, that led to an element of sharp satire rare in decoration, with a keen and sometimes sinister edge not seen again until Art Nouveau.

The Chinese influence in the late seventeenth and eighteenth centuries caused European decorators to imitate the portrayal of captive small monkeys found on Chinese screens. There was nothing new in this image, and nothing specifically Chinese, for portrayals of monkeys in human clothing either as satire or as illustrations of real captive animals predate Breughel; but singerie – the fashion for painting grotesque monkeys, dressed in the height of European sartorial elegance or Oriental robes, in the place of people in domestic, urban or rural surroundings – became a French speciality, and owed its development more to mockery than to charming, humorous decoration.

Many European painters had become contemptuous of the Chinese fadism of the aristocracy and wealthy bourgeoisie and the bastardised,

neo-Chinese forms of lesser chinoiserie. At first, it had appeared that the easiest things to display had been those of Oriental origin:

'... their purity of taste and brilliancy admits of their braving every contact. Francis I admitted them, notwithstanding his admiration for the works of the Renaissance. Under Louis XIV the furniture and porcelain of China and Japan were associated with ivory and bronze to relieve their severity. Their part in decoration gradually increased in the following reigns, and at the end of the eighteenth century became dominant, as we may judge by this description of a boudoir, taken from "Angola", an Indian story, a work contrary to all probability.

' "In a recess stood a silver and rose damask couch, like an altar to the pleasures of the flesh, surrounded by an immense folding screen.

' "The rest of the furnishings complemented it perfectly: consoles and cornerpieces in jasper; Chinese cabinets filled with the rarest porcelain; the mantelpiece laden with potbellied grotesques in the most farcical and novel postures; fretted screens, and so on ..." Agra (Paris) 1746.

'Yes; such was precisely the buffoonery and luxury of a gallant and frivolous age rushing with heedless mirth into the gulf which was to swallow it up. Neither the hidden sarcasms, like those of Angola, the remonstrances of austere philosophers, or the honest efforts of Louis XVI, could arrest the fatal leap, and bring back taste and manners to more reasonable paths.'[6]

Singerie enabled artists to lampoon some of the more tasteless excesses of eighteenth-century fashion and their sillier, more pretentious patrons. Monkeys in silk dresses and brocade britches frequently grinning fatuously or with greedy gaping mouths and bared teeth are particularly fine in the work of Christopher Huet, Alexis Peyrotte, and Alexandre-François Desportes. One is reminded of the Ancient Egyptian Armana

6 Albert Jacquemart, op.cit.

Fig.13
English Chippendale screen (two panels)
c.1760
Hand-coloured paper mounted on fabric
in wooden frame
100 × 90 cm (39½ × 35½ in)
Courtesy of Stair & Company, London

period satires, showing a baboon pharaoh struggling to control a wayward chariot team.

As painted decoration became more popular than lacquer in the 1730s, the scope for artists to satirise chinoiserie increased enormously. Screens with Chinese human figures *and* monkeys together, playing as man and beast, gave way to the monkey becoming the same size as the man, then replacing him or a lady in his company. Eventually the monkeys took over.

The most common activity depicting monkeys showed them playing musical instruments – violins, bagpipes, flutes and timpani; they might also be seen experimenting at the keyboard. Often, as in Peyrotte's famous singerie six-panel screen of 1760 at Waddesdon Manor, England, they are seen in the company of other subservient or captive creatures, usually birds: swans, herons and storks. They may lead hunting dogs. Cats – who were also the verbal or visual equivalent of a veiled insult when applied to a man more often than a woman – could appear as equals of the monkeys, either giving or taking written lessons at desks. Twentieth-century screens in the singerie style (figs 56, 57) usually display a lighter, less aggressive appearance than their predecessors.

Singerie made fun of the fashion for all things Chinese. Many Western artists had, of course, produced screens and all manner of decorative objects in entirely European style and fine art itself assimilated what it deemed valuable from the East. Huet, decorating two rooms in the Château de Chantilly – the *Grand Singerie* (a salon), and the *Petit Singerie* (a bedroom) – even portrayed a folding screen covered with vignettes of parasols, dragons, pavilions and pagodas in the background, and in the foreground a group of monkeys in mob caps attending on an aristocratic monkey at her dressing table.

A Definitive Decoration – Paper-Covered Screens

Chinese wallpaper had appeared in Europe in the last decades of the seventeenth century. Throughout the eighteenth century – the golden age of the folding screen – it not only remained highly desirable but was to develop, especially in France, into one of the leading materials of decorative art.

'China paper' was not attached directly to the wall. As a result, papers have survived which would have been long lost if they had been glued to the surface of the building. 'Hanging paper', as it was also called, was reinforced by a backing of canvas or linen, which, in a manner similar to an oil painting, was then stretched and hung on a frame. This wooden frame was attached to wooden pegs which were driven into the wall, allowing air to circulate so that the paper did not become mouldy, or tear when the wall cracked.

Exactly the same method was used to mount wallpaper on 'India or China' screens, and usually it was the same artisans who carried out the work. The paper itself was very costly, second only to fine silks, and the original Chinese papers came in three categories: figures in landscape, industry, and the flora and fauna of the natural world. In the mid-1700s, those portraying industry were the most expensive at seven shillings a yard (in an age when a soldier earned sixpence a day), but fourpence could buy a yard of trees and flowers.

The birds, trees and flowers of this paper were usually portrayed with such exactitude that their species could be precisely identified. Generally, the design was arranged so that there was a gently undulating ground at the base of the screen and the foliage spread upwards from a central position on each panel, with birds perched in the branches or in flight between them. The plumage of the birds was brilliantly coloured, and the background tints were normally a soft blue or 'pea green'.

The costly papers depicting the working life of China were hand-drawn and painted like those of the birds, despite printing having long been known in China. On the rare occasions when papers were printed the figures were produced in outline – a printed paper shows the indentation around the edge of the form – and were then hand-coloured with either tempera or gouache.

A charming two-panel Chippendale screen of c.1760 (fig.13) reflects the grace and clever simplicity of the paper-panelled screen. Hand-coloured Chinese prints or drawings demanded a lighter frame than the rococo fantasies of many other screens, and the spareness and crispness of drawings gave the screen a restrained vitality.

Japanese paper screens rarely reached the West. Unlike 'India paper' screens which were 'hung' by craftsmen on arrival, they were ready-assembled objects which could be all too easily damaged in transit. An early eighteenth-century Japanese paper screen (fig.4) displays the intricate hinging of the panels which enabled the painted design to be continued across the gilt leaf foreground; the whole air of lightness, delicacy and extraordinary detail, which never becomes oppressive, makes a compelling contrast to the massive lacquer screens of the time.

European paper manufacturers, however, continued printing wallpapers, generally with increasing success, and wallpaper screens were to reach their peak with the incorporation of French block-printed papers at the end of the eighteenth century, which would picture famous views of the Grand Tour, great natural wonders or the Seven Wonders of the World, a speciality of the great French manufacturers Réveillon, Jacquemart and Bernard, and Zuber and Dufor.

Folding Geography – Map Screens

However, European painted paper and wallpaper screens had been foreshadowed by Japanese paper screens folding like a huge map. The Jesuits, arriving in Japan in the mid-sixteenth century, were acutely aware of the enormous language difficulties which obstructed their attempts to advance Christianity, and the theological significance of the geography of the earth, which appeared to place Europe and the Holy Land near its centre, for the spread of the Faith. It was easier for them to communicate ideas and stories through visual media, and between 1590 and 1630 'namban', a style of art which was a hybrid of Japanese and Western painting techniques, flourished in Japan as a method for teaching and communication. Like most such learning tools, its aesthetic merits were generally mediocre, but the folding screen became the chief vehicle for 'namban'.

Originally used to portray poorly-understood Bible stories, the namban style became more successful in depictions of landscape subjects and for producing maps. A surviving World Map screen dating from early in the namban period, executed in water-colour on paper, is profusely decorated with ships at sea, and portrays the four hemispheres with representations of the Ptolemaic universe in all four corners.

A pair of map screens from the latter end of the namban period (now in the Idemitsu Museum of Arts, Japan) derives from a map of the world

A NEW MAP OF THE WORLD OR TERRESTRIAL GLOBE

Fig.14
English map screen (six panels)
c.1760
Paper mounted on canvas
210 x 339 cm (82½ x 133½ in)
Courtesy of Mallett & Son (Antiques) Ltd, London

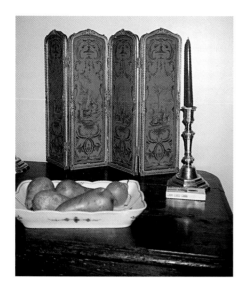

Fig.15
French table screen (four panels)
Late eighteenth century
Painted wood
30 × 45 cm (12 × 17½ in)
Courtesy of Paravent, London

by Willem Blaeu, who based his chart on one produced by the Dutch cartographer Petro Plancius (1552-1622). Plancius divided the world into western and eastern hemispheres, while portraying the northern and southern hemispheres in two circular inner cartouches. The left-hand six-panel screen portrays the western hemisphere, the right screen the eastern. The two outer panels of both screens each portray two vertical columns of people of the world in their costumes, in colour on gold leaf, and the moulding of these 'People of Various Lands' reveals that they must post-date the map, and are probably based on wood-block print figures of the *Complete Pictures of Various Lands* published in 1645. This is the probable source of the cities in other screens of the later seventeenth century, such as an eight-panel screen portraying four great European cities with the costumes of the inhabitants in a frieze above.

A European world map screen of the mid-eighteenth century was an object for reference and decoration – in effect, a complete, flattened-out, free-standing atlas. These maps were hand-coloured paper from copper-plate engravings laid over canvas, and generally pictured the eastern and western hemispheres centrally, then Europe, Asia, Africa, North and South America around the edges. On the margins was other information, the firmament, and views of major cities. Fig.14 is typical, this large six-panel screen showing the whole world literally at a glance. Part of the practicality of this screen is its dado panel, from shin level; charts lower than that would be damaged easily and inconvenient to read.

In England, map screens had become common from the early eighteenth century, and were generally of two kinds: either a simple large map – such as Rocque's plan of London – or an assortment of scrap book engravings. However, there were exceptions, such as the fine Thomas Jefferies four-fold screen (now in the British Library) dated at around 1750. This portrays Africa, Asia and America along with twenty peripheral maps of the firmament and regions of the British Isles, twelve sheets for the countries of Europe, three for parts of the British Isles, and a trio portraying twenty miles around London, Oxford and Cambridge. This screen was not produced for a particular client, so as a selling point the manufacturer marked out the course taken by Admiral Lord Anson's fleet (which captured the famous Manilla galleon) across the oceans. It refers to the South Atlantic as the 'Etheopian Ocean' and to the South Pacific as 'The Great South Sea'.

Although European examples survive from before this date, constant use both as objects of furniture and sources of reference usually destroyed them, even though a typical architectural view or map was generally printed on paper laid over canvas on a pine screen-frame, to give it durability. However, the use and occasionally the 'mis-use' of such screens is well recorded in imagery of this period. The notorious screen in Sheridan's *The School for Scandal* (1777) was a map screen; the map appears to have been double-sided, with maps of the world on the verso and those of Europe (and, doubtless, England in particular) on the recto.

Many map screens, however, were one-sided, their charts all on the front. In all their variations they were deemed 'useful and entertaining Screens for large Rooms, Halls and Counting houses'.[7]

Tea and Table Screens

The English, more than any other nation in Europe, took tea. It was a ritual of great precision, but without the formality the French might have imposed upon it. Crucial to the art was keeping the teapot warm, which required screening it from cooling airs. The table or 'tea screen' is said to have developed as a 'tea cosy' to shield the pot, just as the larger screen shielded the tea-drinkers. The miniature screen might match the larger, as a doll's house might match the decor of the house containing it.

Tea screens may well have begun as design maquettes – miniatures from which craftsmen were to build the full-sized design – but those which survive from the later eighteenth century are versatile objects of table furniture. One might use them to shield any local glare or draught against a candle, to give privacy to a desk, or simply to furnish ornament for its own sake. It is notable that such charming objects reappeared during the 1920s in glass and polished metal under the auspices of the American firm Tiffany, in an age where there was little necessity to 'shield' a pot of tea.

Elegance, Obsolescence and Rediscovery

Seen simply as a piece of furniture, sporting its singerie and rococo conceits, the folding screen ought to have been an immediate casualty of the Ancien Régime's collapse in France after 1792. Instead, some of the finest examples were produced for Napoleon at the Tuileries, replacing the traditional royalist fleurs-de-lis with grand Greco-Roman figures surrounded by Caesarian laurels, the *nouveaux riches* of the empire of equality, liberty and fraternity having quickly usurped Bourbon pretensions. (With the Restoration of 1816 the fleurs-de-lis blossomed again on the same screen panels.)

The motifs of Napoleonic France favoured gods, goddesses, dramatically ruined architecture, allegorical figures or scenic landscapes, all images of the Romantic revolutionary thirst for travel and conquest, crossed with a passion for Ancient Greece (seen in a style then erroneously known as 'Etruscan' which had been launched by the French cabinet maker Georges Jacob in 1780), as well as Egypt and Rome. A flirtation with Turkish opulence and middle-eastern adventure also stimulated extravagant drapings and swags in satins trimmed with lace, folded, pleated and tasselled. All of these things, including panoramic landscapes, appeared on hand-painted wallpapers which had largely supplanted wall paintings in affluent interiors. These were repeated on screens.

During the revolution the firm of the most eminent eighteenth-century papermaker, Réveillon, was taken over by Jacquemart and Bernard.

7 Tony Campbell, *Review for National Art Collections Fund*, 1997, p.84. *Lit:* D. Hodson, *Country Atlases of the British Isles published after 1703: A Bibliography*, Vol.1, Welwyn Tewin, 1984; Atlases published 1704-42 from subsequent editions, 1984, pp.142-82.

Fig. 16
English screen (four panels)
1810
Tempera on paper mounted on
canvas on wooden frame,
depicting St James's Park
176 x 208 cm (69½ x 82 in)
Courtesy of Stair & Company,
London

The PROMENADE

Fig.17
English *découpage* screen (three panels)
Early nineteenth century
Scrap paper mounted on canvas
160 x 210 cm (63 x 82½ in)
Private collection

With Zuber and Dufor, they became the leading manufacturers of wallpapers, and screens – seen as movable extensions of the wall decor – were often covered in these fine papers. By 1810 there were many varieties of papers with geographical and archaeological motifs, often in *trompe l'œil*, which were ideally suited for screens. The figures depicted in these designs were frequently in grisaille against aubergine, dark green or amber backgrounds – colours with a long screen pedigree – and the design on the screen was integrated with the interior architecture.

Scenic papers were very costly, with as many as 2000 blocks to complete a design sequence. They portrayed vistas far and wide, but views of Italy, and 'Monuments of Paris' were typical, while mythical themes like The Loves of Psyche were alternatives. Naturally, a North American series featured scenes from the 1776 revolution, and romantic wonders like Niagara Falls. Sections of these panoramas were used for three- and four-panel screens, and were usually given a border of stylised leaves and flowers. Such papers were not necessarily in full colour, and often lilacs, sepias and creams were preferred, especially if the rest of the interior was in a softer tone.

The early French wallpaper screen (fig.21) by Jacquard and Peyrotte, showing a carriage and postilion outside an estate, typifies the overall design of such screens, with mural format above the faux marble dado panels. The image itself has the luminosity one may see in oil painting and the delicacy often associated with water-colours.

The fabrics previously used for eighteenth-century screens were still used extensively in the early nineteenth century, but their elaborate motifs of acanthus scrolls, floral bouquets and cornucopias gave way to the sparer designs of medallions and geometry to augment Napoleonic symbols – particularly the encircled 'N', eagles and bees. Designs on a six-panel screen for Napoleon himself at the Tuileries (now in the Musée Mobilier and Musées Nationaux) were produced by one of the leading painters of the day, Jacques-Louis David, and the chairs in the rooms closely matched the screen in carving and fabric. This integration of the printed-paper covered screen with architecture, wall-hangings and pictures, and the fabric-covered screen with chairs and furniture, continued in France after the Restoration, the furniture and fabrics becoming more ornate and the colours more strident.

As the nineteenth century approached, the folding screen had dived into relative obscurity in Britain. It is conspicuous by its absence from the great neo-classical style books which record the work of Sheraton, Thomas Hope and Henry Holland between 1794 and 1830. The ghost who had died of symmetry would have shivered familiarly in the Neo-Classical interiors of Regency England. They suggested a cool formality and they were literally cold; indeed, their occupants made little attempt to eradicate draughts as their more informal eighteenth-century predecessors had done. The openness of the grand drawing room of *c.*1800-30 was intended for the reception of company. Its chairs were

Fig.19
Russian screen (four panels)
Early nineteenth century
Oil in canvas on wooden frame, depicting St Petersburg
223.5 x 310 cm (88 x 122 in)
Courtesy of Stair & Company, London

Fig.20
Continental *découpage* screen
(four panels)
*c.*1800
Paper mounted on canvas
185 x 220 cm (73 x 86½ in)
Courtesy of Mallett & Son (Antiques) Ltd, London

Fig.21
Jacquard and Peyrotte
French screen (four panels)
c.1820
Printed paper mounted on canvas
210 x 240 cm (82½ x 94½ in)
Private collection

arranged around the walls in pairs, mirrors reflected light onto a great console, and busts stood on columns in corners. There was no place for a high, folding screen in what was, essentially, a domestic form of the Greek temple.

A four-fold screen such as that painted in 1810 in tempera portraying *The Promenade in St James's Park* (fig.16) is therefore rare. It depicts fashionable strollers in front of Buckingham House before its rebuilding as Buckingham Palace and is signed 'Dreyfus'. A similarly rare Russian four-fold screen of about 1820 (fig.19) – a panoramic view of St Petersburg, painted in oil on canvas – is late in this genre, and is a reminder that fashion never spreads consistently across society or countries. The building to the right is the grotto of the Summer Palace and it is interesting to compare the charm and relative naïvety of this screen with one designed between 1836 and 1839 by Peter Gambs for the Winter Palace, of etched glass set in an ornate gilt frame, which has a monumental quality to match the setting. But in more restrained interiors the painted landscape screen continued in Russia well into the 1830s, in contrast to its seemingly terminal decline in England.

English screens were now usually relegated to a small, relatively informal room or study. The painted silk example of the early nineteenth century portrayed in fig.18 recalls the fashions of the late eighteenth century, which, despite its lightness and delicacy, makes it an object ill-suited for the Greek Revival. But it was nevertheless retained, for in our own age of gross materialism it is easy to forget that in the eighteenth and nineteenth centuries the British rarely threw away any well-made object. In the study, the screen became increasingly a charming and idiosyncratic piece of furniture: the scrap screen. This was made by pasting cuttings from journals and newspapers onto it, either of general interest or on a theme peculiar to the screen's creator. The best known British scrap screen is probably Lord Byron's 'theatre screen', on which between 1811 and 1814 he glued portraits of his favourite theatre personalities, with boxing champions on the verso.

The English *découpage* screen (fig.17), with its agglomeration of figures of earlier times and its eccentric design and robust colouring, is quite different to the continental *découpage* (fig.20) of the same period as Byron's screen, the elegant formality of which bespeaks an object still carrying design prestige.

The Screen's Revival

No Meaningless Ornament:
Victorian Artists' Screens

It was as an art and craft object and later, as part of the ideological reaction to industrialism, that the folding screen survived in Britain, the spearhead country of the industrial revolution. The excessive and oppressive ornamentation frequently associated with the Victorian era was originally marketed to the new visually illiterate British industrial middle class, and was a product of machine manufacture. The use of the machine was perceived to be responsible for what the architect and Gothic revivalist A. N. W. Pugin described as 'meaningless ornament'. In response to this an increasing number of social philosophers such as John Ruskin and others influenced by him, such as William Morris, formed the belief that art was essentially a 'hands-on' craft-based discipline, with its spiritual roots in the antithesis of urban and industrial society.

William Morris (1834-96) saw the folding screen as a vehicle for embroidery and stained glass. His assertion that 'you should have nothing in your house that you do not know to be useful or believe to be beautiful' was fulfilled by the screens produced by Morris & Company, later sometimes in collaboration with the Pre-Raphaelite painter Sir Edward Burne-Jones (1833-98). The great grace and economy of these designs – usually idealised medieval figures set on a background of embroidered flowers or constructed in stained glass set in wooden frames – placed them as exclusive, free-standing objects, in an interior of matching rugs, carpets, ceramics and book bindings.

Typical of the exclusive art-based yet intimate nature of the screen revival in Britain in the second half of the nineteenth century is the extraordinary four-panel screen of about 1869 by Sir Laurens Alma-Tadema, an eminently successful member of the Royal Academy, and his new wife, Lady Epps Alma-Tadema. This six-foot high portrait screen pictured the Epps family (with some potent humour, like spiders over people's heads) dressed in Renaissance costumes, promenading into a room across the screen, while the lower third of each panel, painted in a brick red ground, set out the key of the family's names in illuminated style. The verso is a *découpage* of scrap-screen type set on block-printed wallpaper. In 1859 the father of the young Paul Cézanne bought a large seventeenth-century house near Aix-en-Provence, and his son painted a six-leaf folding screen for this, augmenting a composition of decorative wall panels depicting The Four Seasons copied from Lancret. The screen was two-sided, the verso covered in eighteenth-century portrait medallions and floral designs, the recto an Aix landscape painted to look like an early eighteenth-century tapestry. The figures and the whole composition are slightly naïve. The gulf between this screen and the later works by Cézanne is vast, but its essentially bygone style and its apeing the effect of another medium reveals that the interest in the screen at that time was not forward-looking but nostalgically retrospective. The screen was seen as a 'past object' and an element in the field of 'domestic theatre', a trend which frequently underpinned the creation of deliberately period decor.

Nonetheless, Cézanne's screen, in looking back to a previous period, was the intellectual equivalent of the experiments of the Pre-Raphaelites and William Morris, and Cézanne was not alone. Jean Corot (1796-1875), the most eminent landscape painter in France at mid-century, had also produced a six-panel folding screen in the early 1850s, his collaborators being Charles Daubigny and Armand Leleux, who painted a *trompe l'œil* foliated trellis effect on the outer panels and across the top, while Corot painted a rolling wooded landscape across the centre four.

The impetus of the rococo revival and its significance both in painting and the applied and decorative arts increasingly made itself felt in the homes of the well-to-do during the next twenty years. Elaborate, gilded furniture beautifully worked, and marquetry furniture with grand veneers were increasingly admired on both sides of the Atlantic, inspired by a nostalgic taste for the courts of Louis XIV and Louis XV. 'New money' such as the Rothschilds at their most outrageous promoted it, as in the creation of the famous Rothschild manor of Waddesdon in Buckinghamshire, England, built by Baron Ferdinand De Rothschild between 1874 and 1889. The house was designed by the architect Gabriel Hippolyte Destailleur, and Waddesdon's grandeur, overscaled magnificence and triumphalist message of 'money making all things possible' matched the mood of the new barons of industry. A manifestation of this flaunted wealth was its taste for endless sentimental historicist depictions of the court of Louis XV.

In the context of screens, it is not perhaps entirely coincidental that Baron 'Ferdy' owned a magnificent Savonnerie screen with its panels after Desportes. Gilded screens with swooping rococo shapes began to make an appearance as a background in portraiture, and perhaps nothing better encapsulates this trend than Solomon Solomon's painting of Mrs Patrick Campbell as Shaw's Mrs Tanqueray. She is shown seated in a French interior sumptuously clad in an organza and silk dress, her hand resting lightly on a Louis XV marquetry table, while behind her an eighteenth-century French gilded and carved screen embroidered with Aubusson panels forms a dramatic and stylised backdrop. The painting is typical of the affluent society portrait of its period and its composition echoes the *fin de siècle* grandeur of the age, of which the screen was an integral part.

The weakness of the Tademas' screen – which was never finished – is the lack of concern for how the folding of the panels will affect the design, and shows the artists' unfamiliarity with the medium. Similarly, the young Paul Cézanne's first essay in the medium shows him more interested in the period revival than in the effect folding would have on the completed composition. This is revealing in comparison to the screens of the late nineteenth-century French Nabis group, who considered carefully the effect folding would have on their screens, as did the great American J. A. McNeill Whistler in his famous *Blue and Silver: Screen with Old Battersea Bridge* of the 1870s (fig.27).

On a less exclusive level, by 1850 the urban and suburban middle classes of Britain and the Continent were increasingly occupying houses consisting of modest-sized rooms but accommodating large families. Their furniture was no longer formally arranged and they frequently used screens to create little enclosed areas in a room, a habit not so unlike the partitions used in open-plan offices in the late twentieth century. These screens were frequently no more than plain hessian or wool on a wooden frame, but were often covered in press cuttings, small pictures, woven objects and dolls. Canvas covered with wallpaper was common, while *découpage* made of cut-out prints and engravings on a theme were so popular that domestic journals gave design advice on their effects. These suggested that the creator should bear in mind the relationship between colour and monochrome prints, that one or the other was preferable rather than a mixture, and that subdued or muted tones were preferable in a fully-furnished room. Often one side might be in colour, with the reverse in monochrome, or a dado (or lower third) of each panel might be in colour or black and white, or possibly a chequerboard design. In Britain the best known of these screens is undoubtedly that by Jane Carlyle (the wife of historian and philosopher Thomas Carlyle), probably made in the 1850s, which is now in the library of their Chelsea London house.

Neither was the screen defunct in Italy. A fine Italian four-panel, double-sided, giltwood-framed print screen of about 1850 (fig.22) depicts twenty-two plates from Mario Carloni's contemporary sixty-one plate book *Vestigio delle terme di Tito coloro interne pitture*, which detailed his designs for the restoration of the Baths of Titus in Rome. The book was sold as a fund-raiser for the final restoration (which, with the consent of the Pope, was untaxed). The screen probably had a similar function.

From the 1870s onwards the screen also became familiar in the decor of large Victorian mansions: an object which had seemed an obsolete irrelevance in 1830 had returned as a movable adjunct of Victorian morality, a device for social division. These great houses were very crowded, with family, guests, and sometimes scores of servants. Social propriety generally demanded the segregation of the sexes, except at meals and receptions: large rooms and doors left standing open for the passage of servants could be screened to ensure this. The three- and four-fold screens used for such purposes were often heavily influenced by or were based on French textile designs, which reflected France's renewed interest in eighteenth-century rococo. There was also an infusion of Japanese design following the reopening of Japan to European trade in 1855.

Although period reproduction is so important to the screen market at the close of the twentieth century, it is open to serious doubt whether the French revival of interest in rococo would ultimately have revitalised the folding screen in nineteenth-century Europe without the terrific impetus of the oriental screens which arrived at the end of the 1850s.

Fig.22
Italian screen (four panels)
*c.*1850
Architectural engravings on paper
mounted on canvas in giltwood frame
168 x 169 cm (66 x 66½ in)
Courtesy of Anthony Outred Antiques
Limited, London

A Superb Discovery in Design

It would be wrong to assume that no Japanese art had reached Europe since the Shōgun had curtailed contact with the West in 1650 – there appears to have been a trickle of rare goods and occasional Japanese prints. However, full commercial contact, instigated following Commodore Matthew Perry's official visit in 1853, caused an enthusiasm in Europe which partially overshadowed Chinese art, which had long been familiar. The first major display of Japanese work occurred in the London International Exhibition of 1862 and laid the foundation for an appreciation of the superb graphic skill, as well as quality and craftsmanship, of Japanese goods, particularly impressing Arthur Liberty, whose store consequently became a major retailer of Japanese screens from 1875. The effect of the 1867 Paris *Exposition Universelle* was similar, and many collectors held the opinion of Jacquemart, when he wrote in the early 1870s:

'... the Japanese ware is the more distinguished by the number of its coatings, and the perfection of its polish, which is *non poisseux* – [non-pitchy] – producing the effect rather of a metal than a varnish. The illusion is enhanced by the delicacy of the reliefs in gold, certain pieces looking like burnished iron incrusted with native gold .... In China ... modern objects ... can be readily recognised by their careless execution and the weakness of the varnish. Articles of Chinese workmanship may be known by the feebleness of the goldwork which is more diluted and lacking in warmth, while the ground is less polished, betraying the proximity of the wood. When it was customary to bespeak such work, black lacquer ware was produced in China with scenes scarcely varnished over and everywhere betraying marks of haste and cheap workmanship.'[8]

The damage done by the Tai-ping rebellion (1851-64), which had destroyed major manufacturing centres throughout China, may well have caused this lack of quality in many objects, but Chinese screens continued to be held in high regard by the discerning, and actually benefited from the prestige of the Japanese screens simply because of their many similarities. A carved wood-framed and silk-panelled screen (fig.24), with intricate openwork carving surrounding gold and indigo-coloured silk embroidery of herons in foliage, is typical of high-quality Chinese work in the last quarter of the nineteenth century. It makes interesting comparison with the established style of seventy years earlier seen in the lacquered screen of fig.4. Far more unusual is an English willow pattern screen (fig.23) with a green ground and gilt bronze leather. For a domestic screen this is rare, not only for its quality but for the choice of the famous Willow Pattern motif in these particular materials. In addition it demonstrates graphically the popularity of oriental themes in the upper-middle-class home.

Paradoxically, there is considerable evidence that very few really high-quality Japanese screens were commercially available in Europe, and according to art historian Michael Komanecky a pair of Japanese Kano school screens of the eighteenth century, now in Vienna, were merely pastiches of odd panels (depicting a naval battle) strung together in the

Fig.23
English screen (four panels)
Late nineteenth century
Embossed gilt leather with green ground in the willow pattern
170 x 160 cm (67 x 63 in)
Private collection

8 Albert Jacquemart, op.cit.

nineteenth century. Ironically, too, those first-rate Japanese works acquired were often of the Kano school, which was heavily influenced by Chinese painting.[9]

In the United States, the 1876 centennial exhibition in Philadelphia created an enthusiasm for Oriental screens as vigorous as that in Europe. Although it appears that the quality of many of those on show was not particularly high (the Official Catalogue of 1876 lists screens by Lien Shing and Fow Loong, both commercial Cantonese furniture suppliers, not established artists), by the late 1880s Oriental, and particularly Japanese, silk screens were to be found in every major centre in the United States, not least in the Red Room of the White House.

But the procurement of imported oriental pieces by the wealthy business and social elite was one thing. That in itself did not revitalise the folding screen – such activity was merely the acquisition of beautiful, exotic objects. It was the impression that these screens made on Western artists that ensured the folding screen's vigorous revival in Europe and North America.

Artists had retained the screens in their studios throughout their time in the social wilderness. This habit is typified in a charming genre painting by James Digman Wingfield, inscribed *The Painter's Studio* and dated 1856. The studio depicted is almost the epitome of what might be expected at this period. The painter himself is shown at work at his easel wearing a coloured Flemish casquette that owes much to Rembrandt; scattered about him or lining the shelves are busts depicting Juno, Minerva and various deities from antiquity. Sumptuous rugs and bold damasks are artfully arranged throughout the studio so as to appear randomly scattered. The model herself is shown seated, reading, but with her hair naturally styled and camellias pinned in it, whilst more camellias appear to have fallen at her feet. Behind her is a gilded leather screen of either English or Dutch origin, dating from the 1780s and showing an Elysian scene of game birds disturbed in flight. Importantly, the screen would have been thought antiquated at the time and, with the painting itself, predates any of the interest in Oriental screens that was to become so marked within the next ten years.

About fifteen years later L. C. Henley painted *A Quiet Half Hour* (fig.26): the subject was a lady reposing in a wicker chair, reading a book, backed by sombre seventeenth-century portraits and a Flemish credenza with a copperplate prominently displayed. Rising behind her is a Japanese screen of wooden construction with brightly painted paper panels. These contrast with insets showing traditional Japanese fans, making a pleasing harmony with oriental rugs strewn on the floor. This picture demonstrates how quickly the Japanese screen had become a fashionable adjunct for the upper- and middle-class household and formed an integral part of the interior decoration.

9 Michael Komanecky, *The Folding Image: Screens by Western Artists of the 19th and 20th Centuries*, Yale University Art Gallery, 1984, p.52.

Fig.24
Chinese screen (four panels)
Late nineteenth century
Silk mounted in carved wood
180 x 200 cm (71 x 78 in)
Courtesy of Linda Wrigglesworth

Fig.25
James Digman Wingfield
The Painter's Studio
1856
Oil on canvas
46 x 61 cm (18 x 24 in)
Photograph courtesy of Christopher
Wood Gallery

By acquiring Japanese screens themselves, affluent and influential Western artists began to experiment with the screen again. Komanecky states that in England Sir Laurens Alma-Tadema owned at least ten Japanese screens; Lord Leighton possessed a six-panel one of the Kano school. He also highlights the debate concerning Manet's possible ownership of the screen which appears in his 1868 portrait of Zola.[10] (Manet certainly owned a Chinese folding screen.) Members of the Nabis such as Edouard Vuillard certainly owned screens, as did Alphonse Mucha and Alfred Stevens. Van Gogh may have painted himself one in a Japanese style; it is possible that his portrait of Père Tanguy has this screen as its background.

Above all, however, it was the realisation of how the screen itself could be developed, and the design possibilities which stemmed from these artists' discovery of Japanese art, that mattered. The eighteenth century had copied Chinese art in chinoiserie. The nineteenth century did not mimic Japanese art in the same way, but instead used it far more creatively as a spur to imaginative development.

10 Michael Komanecky, op.cit. p.45.

Whistler – The Screen as Folding Fine Art

How the Japanese screen was incorporated into Western modern art was exemplified in London by two men between 1867 and 1872: the Englishman William Eden Nesfield (1835-88) and the American James Abbott McNeill Whistler (1834-1903). Nesfield was known essentially as an architect, Whistler as a painter. Both men produced screens, and of the two, Whistler's is the more important.

In 1867 Nesfield produced a six-panel double-sided folding screen for the marriage of his architect colleague, Richard Norman Shaw, and it is typical of the financial background of such exclusive work that it was built and carved by James Forsyth, a sculptor of close acquaintance with both architects. The carving was a mixture of authentic Japanese motifs and Anglophile stylisations, while the painting, which made up the central areas of the panels, was in an Anglo-Japanese style of birds and boughs. The pattern on each panel was self contained, however, not continuous as it tends to be on Japanese screens.

The creative circumstances leading to the construction of this screen are also typical of a pattern which emerges in the ensuing period: that of producing an exclusive, experimental decorative object with little or no reference to financial constraint – *ie* the necessity to sell it. This remained one of the main factors dividing the screen as an art object from the screen as a practical if decorative furnishing. However, Nesfield's screen remains essentially art furniture, not a folding art object. Not so Whistler's.

Showman, egoist, sophisticated tonalist and pundit of 'art for art's sake', Whistler was deeply affected by the graphic art of Japan. As a painter rather than a producer of decoration, he painted only one actual screen as an art object, but several times included the painted image of the folding screen in major easel paintings. In these they were not merely an incidental or social detail, but the patterns on the screen and the effect caused by its folding structure became crucial elements in the composition of the paintings.

Whistler's use of the screen in his art can be seen in two major oils of 1864. In *Caprice in Purple and Gold No. 2: The Golden Screen*, the picture holds together on the long vertical lines of the screen folds, across which the reclining horizontal figure of a woman in Oriental costume holding a Japanese print occupies the foreground. The screen pictured is thought to be of the Tosa school with a literary court subject, probably from the Tales of Genji. Whether or not Whistler owned this particular screen, he certainly owned the fine, five-panel Japanese screen he portrayed in the other 1864 oil, *Rose and Silver: The Princess from the Land of Porcelain*. Behind the standing figure of a young woman in a kimono, holding a Japanese fan, this second screen extends to both sides of the canvas. Whistler owned this screen until 1880, when his habitually extravagant lifestyle led to bankruptcy and forced him to sell it. But by then he had made *Blue and Silver: Screen with Old Battersea Bridge*.

The fact that Whistler titled his screen as if it was a painting shows that he regarded it as a folding free-standing work of art – a variable-surfaced painting – and not merely as a picture which happened to be interrupted by a series of vertical joints or a group of separate designs strung together by hinges. It was probably commissioned by Whistler's leading patron of the 1870s, the Liverpool shipping magnate Frederick Leyland, although in the event Whistler retained the screen until his death. It is a two-panel, double-sided folding screen, the rear face having two non-continuous flower and bird paintings by the Japanese artist Nampo Osawa (*b*.1845) which she painted in a rather Chinese style in water-colour on silk.

Whistler's front-face panels, done in coloured washes of verdigris blue

Fig.27
James Abbott McNeill Whistler
*Blue and Silver: Screen with Old
Battersea Bridge* (two panels)
1872
Tempera on brown paper on canvas
190 x 182 cm (75 x 71.5 in)
© Hunterian Art Gallery, University of
Glasgow, Birnie Philip Bequest

Fig.28
Odilon Redon
Pegasus: Le Paravent Rouge
(three panels)
1905-8
Distemper on canvas
173 x 234 cm (68 x 92 in)
Collection: Kröller-Müller Museum,
Otterlo, The Netherlands

and deep green in tempera on brown paper mounted on canvas, show a pier and part of two spans of the old wooden Battersea Bridge. The golden full moon is just under the line of the outer span, the lighted clock tower of the old Chelsea Church counter-balancing it under the centre span, and the hazy form of the partly-built Albert Bridge can be seen in the background. Whistler's charcoal sketches for this composition show that he simplified the structure of the central bridge pier and aligned it on the central fold of the screen. The weight of the pier is on the left hand panel, allowing for the crucial fact that to stand up, the screen panels must be angled forward or back, naturally altering the perspective of the composition. This deceptively simple bridge shape therefore swings gently towards the observer or away, depending upon how the screen is bent, but never loses its basic form.

The great significance of Whistler's screen (apart from its obvious acknowledgement to Sino-Japanese painting) is as an experiment in producing a folding fine art image, not merely a series of decorative images arranged on a folding surface.

The Nabis: Folding Perspectives

This achievement of a unified folding image was exemplified by the work of five French artists during the 1890s and early 1900s: Odilon Redon (1840-1916), Armand Séguin (1869-1903), Edouard Vuillard (1868-1940), Pierre Bonnard (1867-1947) and Maurice Denis (1870-1943). The last four were members of the Nabis group.

Redon was of an older generation than the others, but affiliated to them by their admiration for his work. He made at least sixteen screens, many single-panelled, but most of the folding ones have been lost. *Pegasus: Le Paravent Rouge* (finished 1908) is a surviving masterpiece commissioned in 1905, and portrays the escape of the winged horse, Pegasus, from his captor Bellerophon. Redon had painted and drawn this subject many times, but in *Pegasus* it turns almost to expressionist abstraction, the swirling red field with its greyish-verdigris intrusions being an impression of what Redon had felt at the sight of the Swiss Alps, 'which I undoubtedly … stored in my subconscious'.[11]

It has been observed that Redon frequently chose mythical subjects so that his fantasy compositions (near abstractions) would give observers a foothold into something recognisable. Pegasus himself appears in the upper half of the third (right-hand) panel, and the screen 'reads' from left to right. Its preferred position is with both the left- and right-hand panels pointed forward, and is an object lesson in using three panels specifically as a compositional device to draw the observer 'into' the screen – the visual equivalent of stereo sound – so that the colour and space of the image wraps around the onlooker. Such manipulation of the observer's sense of space was a major preoccupation of the Nabis.

By contrast, in 1900 the then young Swiss artist Paul Klee (1879-1940) produced a magnificent five-panel screen portraying the landscape of the

11 Odilon Redon, letter to his patron André Bonger, 3 March 1908; and Michael Komanecky, op.cit. p.82.

64

Aare river valley. Klee made no attempt at continuity across the panel folds, but rather reproduced on each panel the tall, narrow format landscape illustrations familiar in many periodicals of the time, in strong, dark, muted tones. Viewed in toto, the screen's effect bordered on abstraction, since the viewer saw effectively the same landscape from five different angles simultaneously as part of one overall design. This was a fundamental principle underlying cubism, which was to emerge nearly two decades later.

Séguin's four-panel screen of 1892, *The Delights of Life*, is relatively conservative in comparison. Strongly Gauguinesque in style, it portrays drink, cards, smoking and billiards on one panel; music and dancing on the next; food on the third; and sex on the fourth. But all four panels appear as a continuous swirling jigsaw of colour, and it seems possible this characteristic influenced Bonnard's fine *Promenade* screen of 1896.

Promenade was Bonnard's second folding screen. It is a four-panel Parisian street scene, with a line of black horse carriages forming a type of background frieze at the top of the screen panels, while the figure of a nanny and her two small charges playing with hoops occupies the foreground, their figures placed in the third and fourth panels. This design could be folded so that the different elements of it came forward or retreated depending on which leaves of the screen were pointed forwards or backwards. Two years later Bonnard produced lithographs of these panels, forty of which were finally mounted on screens in accordance with the Nabis' belief in producing decorative art objects for practical domestic use.

Bonnard designed many screens, while his fellow Nabis Edouard Vuillard had even greater familiarity with the practice, having first produced folding screens to provide privacy in his mother's dressmaking shop – a subject of a number of his early paintings. The sophistication of his later screens reduced forms almost to abstraction and also varied the effect of perspective, a figure appearing to be in the middle distance when the screen was flat, near when the panel was angled forward, and far off when it was angled backwards. This illusion was also present in Denis' beautiful 1902 *Screen with Doves*, the focal point of which varies in relation to the layout of a zig-zag fence.

The belief of the Nabis that their work should enhance everyday domestic interiors was close to the aspirations of William Morris three decades earlier, but their whole approach was dramatically different, essentially because they were inextricably bound up in the Paris art world and the very fine art nature of their product was subsequently reinforced. In the work of the Nabis is found the implicit paradox of the aspiration to produce a practical object which can transcend into an art object. That numbers of their screen panels were later remounted as wall paintings, and that lithographs of them were issued separately or as wall sets, underlines this.

Fig.29
Liberty screen (three panels)
c.1900
Stained oak with incised decorated panels depicting stylised poppies
173 x 153 cm (68 x 60 in)
Courtesy of The Antique Trader at The Millinery Works, London
Photograph: Jefferson Smith

Fig. 30
Leather and needlework screen
(three panels) *c.*1902
The needlework design is taken from a 1901 painting by Peter Behrens
167 x 162 cm (66 x 64 in)
Courtesy of The Antique Trader at The Millinery Works, London
Photograph: Jefferson Smith

In the United States two first-rank painters also experimented with the folding screen at the turn of the century: Thomas Wilmer Dewing (1851-1938) and Albert Pinkham Ryder (1847-1917). Although Dewing's screens are held in high regard because they are the work of an artist of considerable stature, they are equally interesting in what they reveal about American cultural associations concerning the folding screen at that time.

Dewing's clients, occupying East Coast mansions, aspired to traditional Western European motifs, often with strong classical associations, and Dewing produced designs appropriate to this decor. His most frequent format was the standing or seated classical female figure singly occupying one full-length screen panel, three figures to a three-panel screen. Usually these self-contained figures were connected across the panels with a foliage motif. His execution of his screens was quasi-Impressionistic, while the redistribution of the foliage had Japanese resonances.

Ryder, too, produced the decorous female figure in landscape, typically using eccentric work methods in his oil paint on leather screen panels, which have predictably suffered heavy cracking.

While both these artists evidently found the screen format worthy of experimentation, neither produced work of the same significance or confidence as the Nabis, or of the conceptual sophistication of Whistler, and only later, in the work of Charles Prendergast and Thomas Hart Benton in the 1920s, did fine art and the painted screen successfully come together in the United States.

If the Oriental revival had stimulated the acquisition of screens in the United States during the 1870s, it had appeared in the work of artists in Scandinavia. Carl Larsson, who has some claim to have popularised the lightness, simplicity and modernity of the Swedish interior, included Oriental screens in two portraits which he painted at his home in Dalarna, central Sweden, between 1890 and 1910. One, of the singer and actress Anna Peterson Nourie, includes a firescreen, but the second, of Gustav Upmark, shows a full-length Oriental screen which forms a decorative background in what seems initially a surprising contrast to the spare visual restraint of the Swedish interior. But there is an aesthetic parallel between the ascetic economy of Japanese decor and Larsson's cool interiors, and the assimilation of this visual language of the Oriental screen is therefore less of a paradox than it might at first appear.

Art Nouveau

Art Nouveau emerged during the late nineteenth century, at a point of balance between the past on the one hand – with its themes of damsels, birds and animals in landscape, presented through symmetry and a mixture of Classical, Baroque and Gothic form – and on the other hand a desire to move forward into a new era. Its fluidity owed much to Japanese art, but its atmosphere of curvaceous sensuality owed more to the 1890s. Unique, too, in decorative art, it became increasingly possessed by an air of melancholy menace, which after the turn of the century made some of its forms sinister to an extent normally only given expression in the fine arts.

Art Nouveau expressed through decoration some of the deep tensions present in Western society. This reached its apogee in the late drawings of Aubrey Beardsley (1872-98). But in the decorative screen the symmetric leaf forms and dreaming ladies of the earlier Arts and Crafts movement became contorted into swirling metamorphoses. As Janet Adams has commented, hair and tendrils became interchangeable, peacock tails and the long robes of hooded figures one and the same.[12] Similarly, the monkeys of the eighteenth century became spiteful wild apes; foxes, owls, bats and serpents suggested malevolence; swaying lilies, orchids and poisonous plants supplanted the ferns, acanthus, roses and cornucopias of earlier times.

These excesses are not present in the Liberty three-fold screen of *c.*1900 in stained oak, with its incised decorated panels of stylised poppies (fig.29), but the dark wood, long straight moulding and liquid curvature of the poppies at the top of the form are absolutely typical of Art Nouveau, as is another Liberty screen (fig.31) of the same date. The entwined peacocks and acanthus on the four-fold painted gilt and leather studio screen of 1895 (fig.32) also demonstrate the deep-toned colour preferences of the period, and Art Nouveau screens are among the darkest of any, together with the Chinese Coromandels and the leather screens of the late seventeenth century. Where colour occurs on them it is almost always dense and concentrated, and the use of long parallel verticals – like the tree trunks in the three-fold leather and needlework screen (fig.30) taken from a 1901 painting by Peter Behrens – would have been almost unimaginable in an earlier period.

But there was, intermittently, a lighter side to Art Nouveau, seen, for instance, in the commercial work of the Czech-born designer and lithographer Alphonse Mucha (1860-1944), creator of *The Four Seasons* screen of 1897 and the magnificent *Four Times of Day* screen made in 1900. Mucha saw the commercial value of mounting his vertical format lithographs on screen panels. The first of these two screens carried four personifications of the seasons in the familiar female form amid foliage of the time of year; the concept was highly traditional but the execution was in the lighter Art Nouveau manner. The second screen was remarkable not only for the seductive grace of the lithographic images but for the extraordinary, almost Baroque foliage of the curvilinear screen frame, which matches the tendrils and sweep of the flora in the lithographs. Both these sets of images enjoyed a huge renaissance in the 1970s through Athena posters, mounted on thousands of bed-sit and suburban house walls. To the general public of that post-war generation, they *were* Art Nouveau.

12 Janet Adams, op.cit. p.128.

Fig.31
Liberty-style screen (three panels) *c.*1900
Oak with fabric panels
175 × 165 cm (69 × 65 in)
Courtesy of The Antique Trader at The Millinery Works, London
Photograph: Jefferson Smith

Fig.32
A Studio screen (four panels) *c.*1895
Painted and gilt leather depicting entwined peacocks and acanthus
174 x 204 cm (68½ x 80½ in)
Courtesy of The Antique Trader at The Millinery Works, London
Photograph: Jefferson Smith

Darker, less traditional themes dominated many of the carved wood, glass, copper, vellum and painted screens of the Turin exhibition of 1902. Foremost among the exhibitors were the Italian Carlo Bugatti (1856-1940) and the Scotsmen George Logan and Jesse Marion King.

Bugatti exhibited two screens, the first exemplifying biomorphic curvaceousness, while the second was extraordinary in its construction. The latter showed Japanese influence in a floral design on its two panels, but the top of the screen was dominated by a huge shield-like disc more than half the height of the screen again, resembling a medallion or armoured sun. This disc was a dominating theme throughout Bugatti's designs and decor, of which his screens were component parts, such as his design for the bedroom of Lord Battersea in London. Indeed, Bugatti and his Spanish contemporary, Antoni Gaudí (1852-1926), moved steadily away from representational decoration after 1902, and Gaudí's designs for the apartment of the Mila family in 1906 were of astonishing originality, the ceilings, walls, doors and furniture all swirling and undulating in asymmetric, biomorphic rhythms. The interior resembles the forms one sees inside marine shells or corals. It contained two six-panel oak and rose-tinted glass screens, two masterpieces of purely abstract form, the panels all of different heights and offering extraordinary variety as they are opened and closed.

In Britain at the turn of the century the centre of screen-making passed from London to Glasgow, primarily due to the influence of Charles Rennie Mackintosh's Glasgow style. Mackintosh (1868-1928) only designed one folding screen himself, and appears to have seen screens as static extensions of his wider architectural designs. However, his Scots contemporaries did not: the folding screens of A. E. Taylor, Herbert McNair, George Logan, Jesse Marion King and Eliza Kerr used stained glass, wood and metal repoussé. Those of Muriel Boyd, Anna Macbeth and B. F. Maitland incorporated embroidered panels. All of them were similar to Mackintosh's designs, which were largely rectangular, but frequently had parts of the design on the front of the panel protruding above the top of the rectangular frame. Areas of the wooden screen were also pierced, so that the screen no longer literally screened what was behind. This is a good example of design taking precedence over function.

In Brussels, the architect and designer Henri van de Velde (1863-1957) would not have approved of the pierced screen – he famously asserted that 'only utility can generate beauty' – but his screens were scarcely utilitarian. Art is not unique in its apologists constantly asserting one principle whilst practising its opposite, but van de Velde's large glass panels at the top of the screen he showed at the Munich Sezessionist Exhibition in 1899 made it an elegant folding windowed wall. It concealed nothing, while the room in which it stood would not have suffered from anything so mundane as a draught. It also required light for its effect, and so needed to be near windows. That was something it shared with the creations of the American Louis Comfort Tiffany. But it was a measure of the screen's renewed importance to interior design that in 1900 Brussels-based Van de Velde should be approached by Berlin dealers to produce screens for clients such as Count Kessler, a commission that resulted in an elegant four-panel white lacquered wood screen with tinted tin appliqués, not rectangular but made up of parallelograms and half-circles, where the wooden frame shapes were more important than the swirling tin Art Nouveau inserts.

One of the most distinctive Dutch contributions to the *Nieuwe Kunst* (Art Nouveau) was batik. The Dutch had been as much affected by the British arts and crafts movement as their Continental colleagues, but batik, a wax-resist process, came directly from their Indonesian colonies. It marked out a number of their screens at the turn of the century.

Gerrit Willem Dijsselhof, Thorn Pryker and Chris Lebeau all used batik in their screens, Lebeau probably producing eleven using this method, the panels sometimes on parchment. The Dutch designs were sometimes simply non-representational geometric decoration of the highest complexity – a technical *tour de force* of batik – or the elegant herons, peacocks and storks so familiar to Art Nouveau. In 1904 Lebeau produced a small three-panel screen only a metre high with the mythological story of Icarus painted in batik on silk. Icarus' flight towards the sun on the front is in dramatic contrast to the serene reverse, but folding and unfolding can reveal the contrast, which is an intriguing exploration of the potential of the folding image. It was an option not previously explored in screen design.

In all the main interior-design exhibitions of the time the screen was an integrated part of the designer's overall concept. It was generally one-and-a-half to two metres high, usually three-panelled, and echoing the motifs of the room. But there was a wide-ranging demand from the middle class for screens in interiors which had not been custom designed, as demonstrated by the catalogues of the famous Austrian bent-wood furniture makers of Vienna, Gebrüder Thonet. Many were simple bent-wood frames with fabric panels, sometimes with cut-out designs in the lower panels, but others had slotted wooden rack-panels at the top for the insertion of prints and photographs – more elegant versions of the scrap screen. But the most sophisticated were suave, curved, three-panel screens with applied or inlaid decoration, including a continuous landscape or coastal scene.

The most innovative Austrian screens were produced by the Vienna Sezession, a group of avant-garde designers and architects formed in 1897. At least three of the most striking screens produced between 1899 and 1903 were by one of the group's founders, Joseph Maria Olbrich. The largest is an eight-panel wood and glass design fulfilling the function of a folding wall separating a music room from a dining room, and reflecting the main architectural features in its design. His colleague Josef Hoffmann's two screens were also dominated by architectural form, one recalling the shape of a Greek lyre, with elements within the

Fig.33
Alphonse Mucha
Savon Mucha: screen-shaped design for soap box 1907
Colour lithographs printed on cardboard
41.9 cm x 61.2 cm (16½ x 24 in)
© 1998 Mucha Trust

America: Craftsmanship and Fantasy

main panels offering a choice of decorative inserts depending on the client's preference. In either case, the flavour of the Austrian avant garde was toward an architectural perception of the screen that had more in common with the Italian Bugatti and Spaniard Gaudí than the Nabis.

In the United States, only isolated architects and designer craftsman pursued the rediscovery of the folding screen with the same attention and ingenuity as those in Europe. Although Thomas Dewing is viewed as America's foremost screen-maker of the late nineteenth and early twentieth centuries and was fully conscious of its role in a wider decorative environment, he tended to produce his screens as part of a traditional decor, such as the two made to stand with Louis XVI furniture in the mansion of Colonel Frank Hecker. In contrast to the innovations of European Art Nouveau, Dewing's work looked backward into the nineteenth century rather than forward into the twentieth.

It was through furniture designers such as Gustave Stickley (1858-1942), Charles Rohlfs (1853-1936) and Charles Greene (1868-1957) that the vitality and elegance of Mackintosh, and the Dutch and German designers, found a mirror in North America. For these men, the

Fig.34
Josef Hoffmann
Three-panel screen
c.1899
Gilded incised leather panels with brass detailing and ebonised wood
156 x 123 cm (61½ x 48½ in)
Courtesy of Royal Pavilion, Art Gallery and Museums, Brighton and Hove
Photograph: Nicholas Sinclair

simplicity of design, integrity of craftsmanship, and concern to produce a high-quality object for domestic use reflected not only a sympathy with William Morris's aspirations but the legacy of the American Puritan aesthetic, which had previously found its expression in the austere elegance of the Shaker tradition.

The New Yorker Stickley travelled in Europe before making his screens, their linen panels reflecting the long-stem floral designs of Mackintosh, set in a dark oak frame, while Rohlfs of Chicago, and Greene, whose clients were on the West Coast, produced three- and four-panelled screens in oak; Greene also produced screens of mahogany, ebony, and stained glass on plain mahogany panels. The Americans eschewed the inlays and appliqués of European designers, celebrating instead the natural qualities of the wood. It is not merely an absence of folding images that marks out their work, but frequently a complete absence of any pattern at all. Cost, not purely aesthetics, played a part in this, for they intended their products to be within financial reach of the middle class; not a concern of many leaders of European Art Nouveau.

Glass, rather than crafted wood, was the medium associated with Louis Comfort Tiffany (1848-1933), famous as a designer and craftsman in lamps, stained glass and vases, and it is evident that Tiffany produced a substantial body of screens, although they are now rare. Usually they were mounted in brass or other metal frames, and were either relatively simple, their opaque panels of softly marbled glass or, more occasionally, in richly toned fruit and leaf designs of the kind most usually associated with glass lampshades. One of the latter was exhibited at the Paris *Exposition Universelle* of 1900.

More unusually, Tiffany revived the tea screen (or table screen), the miniature screen barely a foot high, the alleged function of which was to shield a hot teapot from draughts – an elite form of tea cosy. These enjoyed popularity for their decorative presence, and other makers, such as the Gorham Manufacturing Company of Rhode Island, produced a delightful version in sterling silver, resembling a three-panelled cigarette case.

Painters rather than designers, Robert Winthrop Chanler (1873-1936) and Charles Prendergast (1863-1948) typify two peaks of achievement in America's disjointed involvement with the folding screen. Between 1910 and 1925, these two artists produced a series of striking pieces. Chanler, whose name has now fallen into undeserved obscurity, had trained in Rome and at the Académie Julian in Paris where the Nabis had studied a little time before, and where he acquired a Japanese lacquer screen at the Place St George. His resulting designs were of the exotic Franco-Oriental type, which he exhibited with great success at the Albright Knox Gallery in Buffalo, and later at Wannamaker's in New York. His work found its way to such customers as Gertrude Payne Whitney and the Colony Club.

The brother of better-known Maurice Prendergast, painter and printmaker Charles Prendergast began his career as a frame maker, and did not begin painting professionally until he was fifty. His screen-making was probably stimulated by Chanler, whose screens he appears to have seen at the 1913 Armory Show. Between 1916 and 1920 he produced probably the finest of his folding screens, painted and gilded, the design being an amalgam of Persian miniatures and American folk art: winged, riding, haloed and seated figures cover the recto of the screen's three panels in an Eden-like setting, with full-sized standing angels on the verso. The whole work has an air of mystery and poetic charm, with the intensity of an illuminated scroll.

Yet these two artists could not really be said to have influenced the development of the folding screen in North America, there being no continuous involvement with the screen as in Europe. It was not until Donald Deskey, in the 1920s, that one can trace continuous development (fig.39), and then it came as a response to a different era.

Omega: The Gaiety of Determined Evil-Doing

In July 1913 the Omega workshops opened at 33 Fitzroy Square, London, at the instigation of the painter and critic Roger Fry. His aim had been to use the aesthetic principles of Gauguin and Cézanne in the applied arts, under the umbrella of a studio where young artists could sell their work anonymously under the Omega name.

Although Omega might seem to be the successor of William Morris in its principle of producing artistic furniture, pottery, carpets, curtains and decorative painting, it differed profoundly in practice. Like Morris, Fry wanted to bring the artist and designer into a close relationship, but Fry saw the artist as far more than a craftsman following a past-orientated principle of truth to materials. And the artists themselves – Wyndham Lewis, Fry, Clive and Vanessa Bell and others – had a totally different attitude from Morris to society and the role of art. Their work was confrontational, their customers a progressive and very affluent minority, and their view of the screen was as a folding modernist or Post-Impressionist painting, either as part of an interior or as an object in its own right. They also had a strong literary connection – Lady Ottoline Morrell, Lytton Strachey and Virginia Woolf were all founder members.

There are six major Omega screens. Duncan Grant's *The Blue Sheep Screen* (1912) and the *Lily Pond* (1914); Roger Fry's *Provençal Valley* (1913); Wyndham Lewis' *Circus* (1913); and Vanessa Bell's *Bathers in a Landscape* (1913) (which was almost certainly modelled on Cézanne's large picture *Bathers* of 1898) and the much later *Music Room Screen* (1932).

Grant's two screens are remarkable. *The Blue Sheep Screen* – with great bright blue sheep – owed much to Matisse's painting *La Danse*, but the *Lily Pond* was soon (in)famous, not merely for its 'bad taste colouring'.

Unlike a painter such as Monet, whose big impressionistic lily pond pictures were perspectively a conventional portrayal of a horizontal water surface, Grant had taken what was a vertical view downwards onto a lily pond, nearly abstracted it, and then turned the surface vertically up in front of the observer. This image was painted in conjunction with a series of rectangular dining tables designed by Roger Fry, on which Grant painted similar whirling patterns; in effect, horizontal lily-pond tables. With its near abstract swirls of black, yellow, red and green the *Lily Pond* screen was extraordinary for its time and could easily have been painted at any subsequent period until the 1970s.

Despite their professed commitment to the interaction of art and life, the Omega artists were anathema to the descendants of the Aesthetic Movement. In *Brideshead Revisited*, Evelyn Waugh sardonically described undergraduate Charles Ryder's discovery that his Omega workshop screen would carry no credibility in his Oxford rooms in the early 1920s.[13] Grant and Bell in particular remained favourite subjects of critics and reviewers, Grant continuing to paint screens

13 Evelyn Waugh, *Brideshead Revisited: The Sacred and Profane Memories of Captain Charles Ryder*, Penguin Modern Classics, pp.29-35.

throughout his long career, and although the Omega workshops disbanded in 1919 their repercussions were considerable. Their legacy remained in the famous 'Music Room' installation at the Lefebevre Gallery of 1932, designed by Grant and Bell. This included a Bell screen of three female musicians, their naked Matisse-like forms holding traditional musical instruments on a low, round-topped three-panel format.

By that time the full force of Art Deco had blown through the decorative arts, and although that movement was thought of by many as modernism, its interest in the folding screen, and especially its fresh approach to the lacquered screen, was in considerable part a result of the popularity of the painted and Oriental Coromandel screen as seen again in the work of Larsson, and the studios and houses of the clients of such artists as Laura Knight (1877-1970) and Glyn Philpot (1884-1937). Knight's self-portrait of 1913 depicts her painting a nude model in front of a scarlet canvas screen, the use of the figure against the red being as stark as that of the figures in Eileen Gray's famous *Le Destin* screen of the same year. Working in the 1920s and 1930s, Philpot took his sitters almost exclusively from the *haut monde*, especially his female subjects, and the presence of the Coromandel screen is striking in such work. In 1927 he painted one of his particular patrons, Mrs Henry Mond (fig.41) (a picture thought daring by the conservative standards of the Royal Academy in 1927, as the society sitter was sitting on the floor) but Philpot used the screen's impressive height and subtle tones of taupe, grey and brown to offset the splashes of colour in the blue drape and pink cushion as well as the unusual pose, which the costly status of the screen contradicted. The same screen appeared in at least two other portraits, those of Lady Packe and Loelia, Duchess of Westminster. A 1935 portrait of Lady Benthall used what Daisy Philpot described as a 'Spanish screen', lifting the picture's conventional society nature to vivacity by means of the screen's striking design. Where the Omega artists had indulged in 'determined evil-doing'[14] with Lily Pond screens, Art Deco would absorb both the modernist vitality of such experiments and the establishment exclusivity of the lacquered Coromandel.

Art Deco

The term 'Art Deco' was coined at the great 1925 Paris *Exposition Internationale des Arts Decoratifs*, itself a watershed in interior design and the design of the folding screen in particular.

The huge show was the first in the century dedicated entirely to the decorative arts, and had been postponed from 1915, when it had been given the *coup de guerre* by World War One. Both the term Art Deco and the show encompassed two contrasting styles: the traditional and modern. The traditionalists were led by designers such as the Frenchmen Jacques Emile Ruhlmann and Jean Dunand, makers of superb screens in which the emphasis lay on exotic woods and materials and, often, labour-intensive craftsmanship. The modernists were headed by Ludwig

14 Richard Shone, *Bloomsbury Portraits*, Phaidon Press, 1993, p.99; and Janet Adams, op.cit. p.157.

Mies van der Rohe (1886-1969) and the British Isokon firm, advocates of mass production, machine-made materials, and sleek, clean profiles. Van de Rohe's minimalist designs for one of the pavilions were considered so obnoxious – 'inappropriate' – that the organisers wanted a twelve-foot wall built around it, and in fact such styles which are often thought to epitomise Art Deco were not widely adopted until the 1930s.

Although the exhibition was officially international, it was dominated by leading French or French-based craftspeople, and their work notably reflected the revival of lacquering, which underwent a renaissance during the first three decades of the twentieth century. Its lustre and depth achieved the same sumptuousness as in the seventeenth or eighteenth centuries, but the treatment of the designs incised into it was utterly different.

Jean Dunand (1877-1942), a Swiss who had resided in Paris since 1900, excelled in the technique and had studied under the Japanese master Sougawara. Dunand is credited with reintroducing the Oriental technique of inlaying minute particles of crushed eggshell into the lacquer surface. Many of his screens were collaborations with Francois-Louis Schmied, Paul Jouve and Jean Goulden. Most frequently Jouve and Goulden drew the designs which Dunand transposed into lacquer, while other designs reflected the inspiration of Robert Delaunay (the 'decorative cubist') and Japanese, Egyptian and African art.

The colours of these screens are typical of the Art Deco age: 'tango' (a deep reddish-brown colour used against black – which was still the most common background tone), ochres, olive, and dark green. In contrast to the modernist machine production philosophy, these colours were created in the hand-applied lacquer, using vegetable dyes.

This 'hand-crafted Modernist' style was responsible for the well known 1925-6 masterpiece *The Battle of the Angels* by Dunand and the Russian Jean Soundbinine. It comprises a pair of three-panelled lacquer screens: *Fortissimo, Screen of Soaring Angels* and a second, *Pianissimo, Screen of Fallen Angels*, with deep blue-green backgrounds dusted with gold. The angel figures are moulded in the Japanese manner of gold-coloured high relief, while angular gold and brown box- or lozenge-like skyscrapers rise below them. Crushed eggshell clouds swirl in scrolls behind them. Built for the music room of one of Mr and Mrs Solomon Guggenheim's houses at Port Washington, New York, it was part of a project to alter the decor of a house, which was 'abominably decorated in machine-made furniture'.[15] The repeated use of this phrase footnotes as many screen commissions and observations of this time as it had in the days of William Morris and his contemporaries seventy years before.

Eileen Gray, one of the most important artists and designers of the twentieth century, who also studied under Sougawara, exemplified the paradox of modernist aspirations expressed through the use of traditional materials. While she rejected the term Art Deco herself, and

15 Rowland Burdon-Muller, letter to the Metropolitan Museum of New York, December 1971.

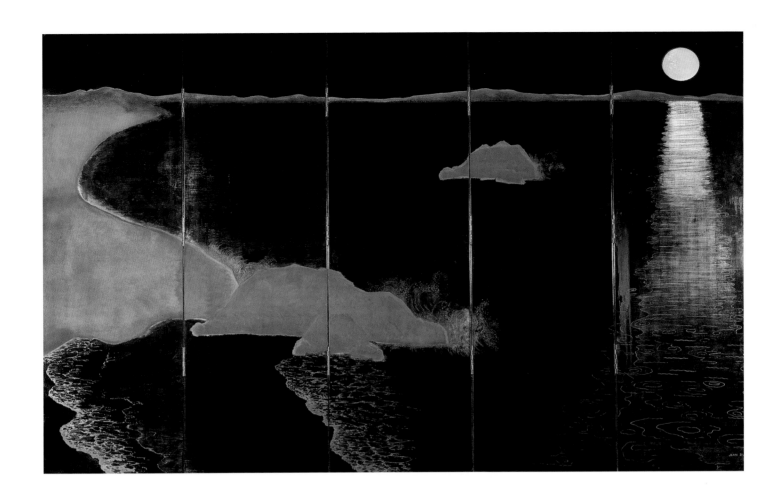

Fig.36
Jean Dunand
Clair de lune (five panels)
*c.*1928
Black lacquer with silver incisions
coarsened with rough earths
62.5 x 225 cm (24½ x 88½ in)
Courtesy of Royal Pavilion, Art Gallery
and Museums, Brighton and Hove

saw her screens as part of an architectural whole with the building, she wanted both the technique of lacquer to be divorced from 'any associations with Chinese Coromandel or Louis XV furniture',[16] and also sought to produce a style without any historical references or associations with natural forms, a modernism later associated with such artists as Donald Deskey. On the other hand, the actual technical production of her designs was highly traditional, hand crafted and focused towards a sophisticated and exclusive market. If modernism was chic it was also extremely expensive and elitist. It might be a product and celebration of the machine age in its forms, but it eschewed anything to do with machinery in its execution.

Gray produced a number of superb screens in a relatively short time, which are among the most important of the twentieth century. The famous four-panel *Le Destin* of 1913 depicts a youth starting in horror at seeing another carrying a terrible burden of which he is unaware, the two pewter-coloured metallic figures set against a vermilion lacquered ground. This contrasts powerfully with a twenty-eight-panel black lacquer 'block screen' of 1924 (fig.37). Its many small panels or 'blocks' are held together in eight vertical rows like interlocking bricks which hinge in and out, their only 'motif' being their single black tone and their relationship to one another. This screen is a free-standing floor sculpture which explores the light and space between its panels as much as the panels themselves. In an interior, views through the screen of its surroundings were as important a part of the visual experience as the screen itself, and were intrinsically 'part of the object'.

There are at least six variants of this screen in black, and three known in white. The rods connecting the panels vary – one version in the Victoria & Albert Museum has brass rods – and while some variants have no more than three blocks per row, others have as many as eleven. Other screens by Gray are solid five-panel rectangular objects with textured and incised silver or gilt angular decoration, or eight-panel black screens with large rectangular areas of silver leaf.

These screens are part of a body of twenty folding screens which Eileen Gray made between 1920 and 1930; many of them come from her 1922 gallery 'Jean Desert', some of them in lacquer, others in celluloid, metal and cork. The concept of the screen as a 'floor sculpture' is so potent and accessible in her work that it connects directly with the concerns of artists such as Andrew Tye at the close of the twentieth century.

Velocity in Decor

The closeness with which Gray, Dunand and others viewed the relationship of their work to the overall design of interiors and to architecture was synthesised in the rise out of Art Deco of a new profession – the 'interior decorator'.

The interiors which these decorators designed were owned by the same income-groups who had bought or commissioned screens in the late

16 Martin Battersby, *The Decorative Twenties*, Herbert Press, 1988, p.44.

Fig.37
Eileen Gray
Screen
*c.*1924
Twenty-eight lacquered wood panels
mounted on brass rods
189 x 136 cm (74½ x 53½ in)
Courtesy of the Trustees of the
Victoria & Albert Museum, London

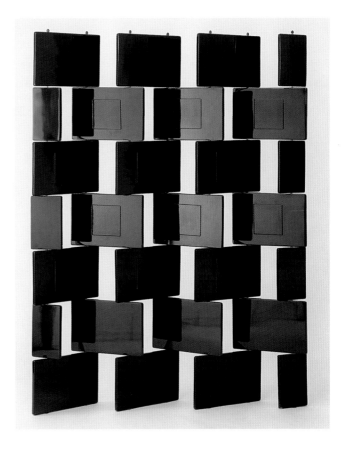

Fig.38
Eileen Gray
Eight-panel screen
*c.*1923
Lacquer and metallic leaf on wood
207 x 432 cm (81½ x 170 in)
Courtesy of the Trustees of the
Victoria & Albert Museum, London

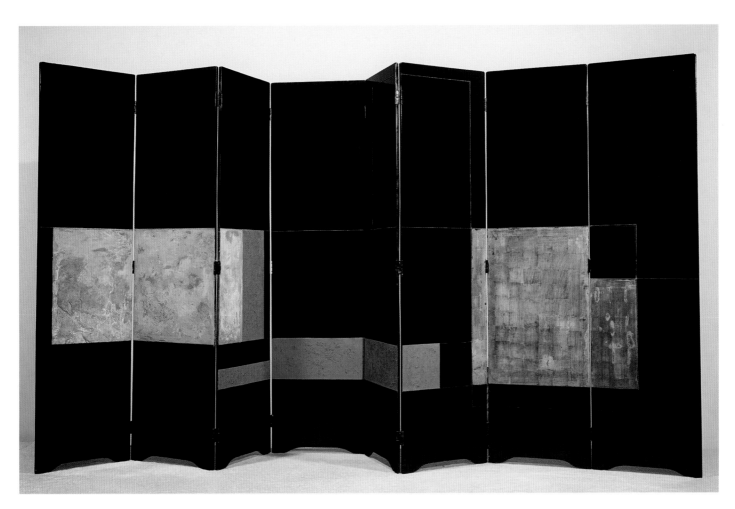

nineteenth century, but their lifestyles had changed. Not only did their establishments contain few servants, but, particularly in the United States, they lived in flats or high-rise apartments. The rooms were often smaller than previously, and the furniture frequently Modernist or built-in. In such places the screen became either an architectural feature (as often in Hollywood films – see p.92) or a smaller furnishing to mask another object, as in the famous Syrie Maugham *White Room*, containing a large glass screen and a low lacquer one to hide the piano.

Dunand, Gaston Priou, Sonia and Robert Delaunay, Donald Deskey and Jean Michael Frank all worked in a wide range of decorative media and it was perhaps inevitable they they should view divisions between these media as technical rather than conceptual. The lacquered, painted, fabric or metallic screen was an object which was a folding painting or a vast piece of jewellery, or a folding extension of a wall. For that 1935 apogee of the modernist age, the Atlantic liner *Normandie*, Dunand's studio – where his son Bernard worked – produced carved lacquer panels twenty-two feet high and twenty-seven feet long, depicting various sports, divided again into lesser sections to avoid cracking from the ship's movement, the screen again finding its way directly onto the wall as it had during the seventeenth and eighteenth centuries. But it was above all as a decorative-art object that the screen re-established itself during the inter-war years, and in the hands of Gray or Deskey could ascend into fine-art sculpture.

Donald Deskey (1894-1989) was one of a group of highly innovative American artists whose fresh and largely unfettered experiments with the folding screen from the 1920s onwards ultimately led to the United States taking the screen further in the ensuing decades of the twentieth century than all but a very few artists in Europe or elsewhere.

A visitor to the 1925 Paris *Exposition Internationale des Arts Decoratifs*, Deskey had become acquainted with the French avant-garde designers, having already founded his own architectural and interior design firm in New York in 1922; he is usually remembered for his distinctive interior decor at the Radio City Music Hall. In 1927 he joined forces with Phillip Vollmer, and went on to become one of America's leading industrial designers, with clients such as Coca-Cola and General Electric. Until the early 1930s Deskey-Vollmer produced custom-built screens, tables, lamps and household furniture in small local workshops, using Deskey's designs. Because they were handmade and exclusive, the number of screens produced was relatively small, and they were painted by Deskey himself, whose love of painting prevented anyone else from executing the designs.

As such, Deskey's screens are an excellent fusion between the formal elements of modern painting, an idiom generally associated with large-scale decorative art, and a functional object. A common feature is the use of a stepped effect produced by building the three panels in staggered heights, the tallest generally on the left. This shape is

Fig.39
Donald Deskey
Design for *Lysistrata Screen*
for Mr Gilbert Seldes
c.1930
Gouache, silver paint and graphite on
illustration board
40.6 × 29.3 cm (16 × 119½ in)
Courtesy of Cooper-Hewitt, National
Design Museum, Smithsonian
Institution/Art Resource, New York
Gift of Donald Deskey, 1975

sometimes associated with the skyscraper images of the 1920s but adds
to the dramatic effect of the angular designs on the panels themselves,
and gives the impression that these zig-zags extend away beyond the
physical edges of the panels rather than being contained within them as
a regular rectangular screen might indicate. A parallel manipulation of
shape can be seen in the works by Piet Mondrian and the De Stijl
painters, whose canvases appear to be 'cut off' geometric fragments
from some larger conceptual whole.

There often appear to be similarities between Deskey's screens and the
concerns of another group of artists: the Cubists and Dadaists of the
1920s. However, unlike them, Deskey had no intention to alter spacial
or surface perceptions, any more than he would allow surface ornament
to distort the integrity of the design.

Fig.40
Albert Rateau
Three-panel screen
c.1930
Oil gilding in silver leaf on burnished
water gilding in silver leaf on white
gesso, with forged iron frame
300 x 240 cm (118 x 94½ in)
Courtesy of Royal Pavilion, Art Gallery
and Museums, Brighton and Hove

From 1913 and the publication of the futurist manifesto, Giacomo Balla (1871-1958) had been experimenting with depictions of landscape and speeding objects in paintings, drawings, and collage. Having worked on the Stravinsky-Diaghilev experiment *Fireworks* he fused the elements of that project of undulating shapes and intense motion in an extraordinary two-panel screen, *Velocity of Lines in Landscape* (1918). One of the panels was a visual rectangle, the other slightly taller and rectangular but with a curved lower outer section. Both front and back were covered in swirling, zig-zag colours like streamers over a beautiful indigo sky, the olive and forest-green curvature of hills and a buff road. This celebrated the motion of a speeding car. When the panels are placed at ninety degrees the effect of perspective and almost visual 'suction' is phenomenal. It is possible that Balla may have intended this screen to interact with two large paintings of a speeding car (visually similar to the screen) so as to portray three moments of the vehicle penetrating the atmosphere. The use of the triptych and its religious connotations recur in Duncan Grant's table and screen and later in Bruce Conner's work and might be seen as implying idolisation of the car in the twentieth century. Using the screen to describe motion in this way may be unique.

Except for Deskey, the only major artist in the United States to produce wholly abstract screen designs during the 1920s was Jan van Everen (1875-1947), whose output included a small two-panel screen mounted in a carved Chinese frame, the frame paradoxically

Fig.41
Glyn Warren Philpot
Mrs Henry Mond
1927
Oil on canvas
146.5 x 135 cm (57.5 x 53 in)
Courtesy of The Fine Art Society,
London

in contrast to the angular abstraction of the artist's work. Both he and his two contemporaries, Carl Newman (1858-1932) and Thomas Hart Benton (1889-1975) were influenced by the ideas of Synchronism (an early twentieth-century style emphasising brightly coloured compositions and abstract forms, developed by the Americans Stanton MacDonald Wright and Morgan Russell) and all three adhered to the consistently American aspiration to experiment artistically within a functional medium. All these artists show the rhythmic and geometric preoccupations found in contemporary paintings. In Van Everen's screens there undercurrents of Kandinsky, in Newman's, Cézanne and Matisse, but in Benton's famous *Screen with Abstract Sea Motif* the fusion of Whistler's Japanese interests, Gauguin's sensuousness and Matisse's decorative organisation all meet in an 'Art Deco' apogee. Benton's four-panel screen shows a near-abstract portrayal of a breaking sea against a navy blue sky with red-brown clouds, a composition frequently compared with Katsushika Hokusai's famous early nineteenth-century blockwood print *The Great Wave of Kanagawa*. This screen was originally designed for a keen fisherman, and the painted area of each panel actually hinges out from the screen's main frame to reveal a shallow niche, into which apparently photographs of fishing expeditions could be mounted – the old tradition of the scrap screen – only this time with the visual pun of the 'trophies' being beneath the waves.

'Screenness' –
The Stage and Film

Fig.42
Attributed to William Hogarth
The Collapse of the Screen
1778
Copper-plate engraving
Courtesy of the Trustees of the
Victoria & Albert Museum, London

The final chapter will look at the late twentieth-century desire to take paintings down from the wall and make them free-standing. This was in fact what the theatre had done for centuries. David Hockney was to state that all theatre flats were basically screens, and that the screen had been an integral part of dramatic art since the Restoration.

By the time Hockney came to design for the theatre in the 1970s, the involvement of the screen on stage and in film had come full circle, and it is useful to survey this before reviewing the further development of the screen during the last half of the twentieth century.

Folding screens had not, of course, been a feature of the Elizabethan theatre. 'How now? A rat? Dead, for a ducat, dead!' shouts Hamlet, and stabs the eavesdropping Polonius through an arras, the hanging tapestry behind which the latter is concealed. In later years it might well have been a folding screen, which became a fine accessory to eighteenth-century drama and comedy, just as it was in the residences of the people who attended the playhouses. Its function had remained remarkably constant over three-and-a-half centuries.

Sheridan's *The School for Scandal* (1777) is arguably the most significant use of the screen on stage in a play that has retained its popularity to the present day. Centred around scandalous gossip and sexual intrigue – 'a serious comedy for trivial people', as David Crane tells it – it is basically about appearances and what they are not, or are wrongly alleged to be – social screens. The convoluted plot begins to unravel crucially in Act IV, Scene 3, when Lady Teazle, a prime subject of the manoeuvrings, is discovered hiding behind a screen. To quote Crane:

'We reach the moment in the play where the physical movement and positioning of characters on stage most vividly picture psychological and moral reality. And no doubt the enormously energetic response of the contemporary audience to the screen scene was because of their recognition that here Sheridan had come to the point where the *trompe l'œil* apparatus of the stage, all its sliding flats and moving curtains, was indeed the natural language in which to describe the society of his day.'[17]

The structure of the screen itself was also important to the workings of the plot, and it has been argued that a certain suspension of belief is necessary as someone hiding behind the screen would logically have been visible at some point to the character of Sir Peter moving about the 'room' of the stage.

According to the stage directions and the apparently reliable 1778 engraving, attributed to Hogarth (fig.42), the 'closet' in which Sir Peter had been hidden was the right hand proscenium door, from which he could hardly have failed to see behind the screen, yet the script makes it plain that he does not. As the screen is not 'four-sided', academics have argued, this scene works because of the quality of the dialogue but not

17 F. W. Bateson (ed.) (amended by David Crane), *The School for Scandal*, A&C Black, London 1995.

the physical probabilities it postulates. By 'four-sided' they presumably mean 'not a rectangle'. However, it should be pointed out that the screen in the engraving is a six-panel structure, and the six-panel folding screen may be positioned in an oblique arc, which would offer the hider concealment from the proscenium door if the screen were not near the curtain line.

The screen itself is a map screen, and that too has affected some modern interpretations of the text. Robert's painting of this scene in the Garrick Club (c.1780) shows the verso of the fallen screen with maps mounted on it displaying the continents – Europe and almost certainly Britain and views of London were doubtless displayed on the recto – and some interpretations of the text appear to feel that maps should be also draped or 'laid over' the screen or in some way festoon it, when Sir Peter says: 'Tis very neat indeed. Well, well, that's proper; and you make even your screen a source of knowledge – hung, I perceive, with maps.'[18]

However, a map screen would naturally be termed 'hung with maps' in the eighteenth century, as the maps on it were paper mounted on canvas on a wooden frame, as one 'hung' a canvas or 'hung wallpaper' (see pages 36, 37, 40).

Performed in the 1780s, *The School for Scandal* was typical of the social comedies of the later eighteenth century, with their props of concealment reflecting the society which had created the golden age of the folding screen. And it was in the theatre house that the screen persisted when it fell into decline in the houses of everyday life.

Looking over the middle half of the nineteenth century, Pierre Larousse lamented the apparent death of the screen, and spoke of 'small drama' as its last bastion. It was no longer used, he said, 'except as a backdrop in elegant theatres to present a proverb or a small comedy that requires very little *mise en scène*'.[19]

This was scarcely surprising. In everyday life the screen had been withdrawn to the bedroom or the study, and it was in such scenes in theatre that it was used. The French farce, descended from the concealment comedies of the eighteenth century, perpetuated it, but it was a prop of no interest in itself, and conceptually it appears almost a tautology that, as an object of the façade *par excellence*, the screen should survive in the temple of façades and appearance – the theatre.

For artists already experimenting with the screen, it was the demands of innovative theatre design at the close of the nineteenth century that led to a vigorous cross-fertilisation first with the theatre, and then with the new potent medium of mass entertainment in the second quarter of the twentieth century – the cinema.

Giacomo Balla's designs for the Diaghilev-Stravinsky collaboration *Fireworks* of 1916-17 resulted in the creation of an angular, swirling

18 ibid.
19 Pierre Larousse, *Grand Dictionnaire universel du XICX^e siècle*, vol.2, Administration du Grand Dictionnaire Universel, Paris 1874.

series of sets where buildings appeared like conical paper darts at all angles of the compass, overlapping with swirling rounded hills which resembled the sweeping curves made by aircraft vapour trails or speedboat wakes. These symbols of speed and mechanical motion on these 'screens' interacted with flashing light effects, whirling shapes and changes of colour directed by Balla, but not incorporating any human dancers. These were later reproduced in his two-panel screen of 1918, *Velocity Lines in Landscape*. Screens were also created by other artists who designed sets for Diaghilev – not least Jean Cocteau, Robert Delaunay, Natalia Goncharova and Jose-Maria Sert.

In 1921, when working on Diaghilev's third ballet, *Pulcinella*, Picasso became aware of the screen's visual exemplification of the theatre as an imaginary world, separated from the real one not by the presence of living people (who are alive on a real stage in the presence of the living) but by their costume, and painted or decorated visual barriers set up between them. His screen, *Two Musicians* (1921), a line drawing painted on cheese cloth mounted on four panels, shows two *commedia dell'arte* characters, Harlequin and Pulcinella, facing each other in the centre panels; Pulcinella has his back to the observer.

Interactions between theatre, film and interior design are typified in Donald Deskey's *Lysistrata Screen* of 1930, a gift to the drama critic Gilbert Seldes, for whom Deskey also designed several rooms. This lacquer and plywood screen portrays Lysistrata, the heroine of Aristophanes' play – of which Seldes was then writing an adaptation – in profile (fig.39) and Deskey's rectangular stepped panel screens, with their elegant geometric forms, were to become archetypes of the Hollywood modernist interior screens of the 1930s. Whether Busby Berkeley choreographic spectaculars or the chic interiors of romantic dramas and thrillers, the Art Deco look was instantly projected into the consciousness of millions of people regardless of the interiors of their own, frequently Depression-struck, homes. The folding Art Deco screen was a powerful prop in these film sets, used particularly to give a sense of height to a room in the same way the towering Coromandel screens would have done two centuries earlier. Their popular step formation – either with the centre-panels tallest and the other, semi-circular topped or square topped ones of descending heights, or a series of descending or rising panels resembling a giant pillar graph – evoked skyscrapers and dramatic modernist (or futurist) architecture. These screens were often illuminated electrically from behind or at their sides, or occasionally across their edges by spotlights or strip neon in the mouldings. Their motifs were Deskey-esque, generally simple, geometric, and they differed from those in real commercial and domestic interiors in that they were usually predominately light-coloured, whereas their privately owned counterparts were generally light and dark in motif. A large dark screen in monochrome film would imply menace, a lighter one status.

To a lesser extent, the screen's presence in the theatre was similar while on a physically much smaller scale, and its function was generally as a realist interior prop or corollary of the dramatic action. The popularity of the screen as an elegant object among the affluent of the 1920s and 1930s was reflected in direct proportion by its use on the film set, which reasserted its popularity and credibility to audiences among both that and less affluent groups. Its decline after World War Two was equally marked in these media.

In film and the theatre, the screen dipped into twilight again in the 1950s. The Hollywood sets of the 1930s and 1940s had belonged to an industry of escapist panache, whereas the 1950s saw the American cinema adjusting to the competition of TV networks and a booming economy of consumers who watched action movies, thrillers and romances set against affluent realism. A screen's only function in a thriller was to hide a body. As a result, it reverted to its nineteenth-century role of theatre prop; if its presence was focused upon, it was at two extremes – either as an image of material wealth and culture, or as French farce: vaudeville comedy.

In the 1957 version of *Paths of Glory* the elegance and comfort of a French general's headquarters is commented upon by one of his divisional commanders in a passing aside as he enters the room and nods toward an early nineteenth-century French tapestry screen. At the other end of the spectrum, the comic prop was exploited by British cinema. Its use as a movable furnishing, supplying opportunities for endless double entendres, is seen at its most obvious in the *Carry On* films, which in *Carry On Nurse* and other heavy-handed medical lampoons probably gave more prominence to the ordinary, functional, metal-framed fabric-covered hospital screen than its manufacturers themselves could ever have done. Vast numbers of undressed people hid behind it, apparently changed sex behind it, were left for years unnoticed behind it. It time-travelled. There is, of course, no record of folding screens being known in Ancient Egypt, but as an ubiquitous comic object it appeared in Queen Cleopatra's bathroom complete with mock hieroglyphics in the *Carry On Cleo* spoof of Hollywood's disastrous 1963 spectacular *Cleopatra*, and, set in a 'Ptolemaic' frame, was the set designer's in-joke equivalent of Julius Caesar wearing a wrist-watch with Roman numerals.

It is ironic that during the 1960s when the screen, as an art object, floor sculpture and medium for pop artists, became a vehicle for vigorous experimentation, in the theatre it was present largely as a device for light period drama, Whitehall Farces, or Gilbert and Sullivan operetta, including, naturally, *The Mikado*. Larousse's remark about 'the Chinaman in the screen' had come full circle.

David Hockney, however, equated all stage flats with the screen. They were, in effect, small and giant variants on the essential form. Those which hinged were different from sculpture and furniture only in so far as they purport to 'hide themselves in their own presence' – that is to say, they are seen as a pair of columns or as a doorway, a trio of pointed-topped temples side by side, or portions of landscape. In his set for Act I, Scene 3 of the 1978 Glyndebourne production of *The Magic Flute*, commissioned by David Cox, Hockney produced a triptych of temples – Nature, Wisdom and Reason – set like a three-panel folding screen, the centre temple set back slightly, the two outer ones angled forward. The central door aperture in the towering truncated pyramid of Act II, Scene 7 also recalls the aperture effect of the diving board of the truncated flat-topped triangle of the bathing pool in the swimming pool screens he made very soon after *The Magic Flute* production. In both cases the artist was concerned to explore the appearance of a surface membrane which could be penetrated or folded back, which is the door-like, flap-like aspect of the movable barrier that one might describe as essential 'screenness'.

Innovation and Restoration:

The Contemporary Screen

Sex, Mandalas and Paper Pools

As a sexual metaphor the folding screen has rarely been used by artists as explicitly as it was from the 1930s to the 1970s. A double-sided, traditionally opaque membrane which folds together intimately, hides what will or will not later be revealed, can appear part of the established structure (a building) but be overthrown or removed, and can be perceived as threatening or inviting, decorative or functional; the screen's Freudian connotations are almost too numerous to name. It is evocative of a couple, separated or together; of a past, present or future relationship; of formality and decorum; of hypocrisy or discretion. Add to this the transparent screen, and one is instantly confronted with voyeurism.

All this was both implied and explicit in previous centuries in the paintings of Watteau and Fragonard, and later Degas, Matisse and others, but in the twentieth century the screen itself rather than its inclusion within a painting became the artist's direct statement of these preoccupations. Neither does a screen have to contain a representational image to be erotic. Perforation is sufficient.

As Virginia Butera has described, Marcel Duchamp's (1887-1968) famous *The Large Glass* (1915-26) – although not a folding screen, but a painting on two glass panels originally mounted one above the other as a partition (*ie* a non-folding screen) – began the explicit pursuit of sexual metaphor.[20] What looks like a coffee mill, attendant apparatus, and splashed pool of coffee is really a view of a rape. The full title of the glass, *The Bride Stripped Bare by Her Bachelors, Even* depicts the stripping and violating of the bride in the upper panel by the nine bachelors portrayed in the lower. As Butera observes, the composition even includes three voyeurs, and this incident takes place 'on' or 'through' glass. She elaborates upon the close connection between this and the 1935 screen by Duchamp's close friend, Man Ray (1890-1978).

Man Ray's extraordinary five-panel screen was originally inspired by a poem by Paul Elouard; the centre panel portrays a naked, svelte young woman pulling a gown over her head – whether up or down is ambiguous – so that her face, breast and arms are obscured. At her feet and stretching to a distant sea is a row of staring eyes like red footlights, while behind her is a fountain with hands holding up other hands rising from it. In the lower left corner is a spiral lampshade lying on the ground, and behind her a comet streaks overhead and drops toward the sea.

Painted on an object traditionally used to hide a woman's body from a man, this screen is potently provocative, almost a paradigm of masturbatory eroticism. The low-level eyes evoke a strip-tease audience, and the hands, which imply touch and reaching out, are held and restrained by other hands. The meteor-sperm falls away into the collective ocean behind her. That she is strip-teasing is reinforced by the obscuring cloth tangle of her upper body, which, as Whitney Chadwick argues, embodies 'the surrealist duality of desire coupled with fear of castration'.[21]

20 Virginia F. Butera, 'The screen as metaphor', *The Folding Image*, Yale University Art Gallery, 1984, p.207.
21 Whitney Chadwick, 'Eros or Thanatos: the surrealist cult of love re-examined, *Artforum*, no.14, November 1975, pp.46-56.

The legacy of the surrealist found object and the folk art of the scrap screen came together in Bruce Conner's work in the 1960s. Conner, then working in Mexico City, conceived a three-panel screen to divide a room and complement his dining-room table, on which he had painted a composition of the Last Supper. The tops of the screen panels were pointed, as they might be on the sections of a medieval triptych altarpiece, and Conner occupied the place at the table amongst his guests which on the table-top was filled by Christ. The screen bore popular Mexican prints of Christ, and Conner placed candles on its top corners. The whole performance of this symbolism in a strongly Catholic country might be seen as deeply blasphemous, or at least highly aggressive, but the screen was only at its 'opening' stage and the artist continued to amend it as he moved around the United States. The overtly Christian religious images were mingled with the sartorial aspects of commercial sex – prostitution – or the ordinary ornamental and clothing accessories traditionally associated with women, until a vast sheaf of nylon stockings cocooned the screen with ribbons, pieces of broken mirror, hair and broken costume jewellery. The greatest accumulation of these things is on the back of the screen, where one would traditionally undress, and a deliberate patina of dust covers them all. The whole grotesque monstrosity evokes the perished remains of victims or some spider's web or egg cocoon, but seems to imply either an uneasy alliance between the two great forces in society, religion and sex, or, conversely, a complete contrast. The recto of the screen has a predominance of religious imagery, the verso sexual, underpinned by the screen's title, *Partition*.

The Englishman Allen Jones (*b.*1937) first became interested in folding screens in 1959 as a result of seeing one in a corridor of the Victoria & Albert Museum while he was a student at the Royal College of Art. The narrative content of the panels implied a simultaneous passage of time and space and this affected his 1965 screen, while its predecessor of the year, *Female and Male Diptych*, partially inspired it as the two panels were originally placed so that both the man's and woman's feet were resting on the studio floor (they are not in the finished position of the diptych). The upper areas of both pieces are dominated by vivid diamond-shaped Jungian mandalas. In the screen there are two of these, one containing one and the other two pairs of female lips, while in the Diptych one mandala contains female lips and a male sperm like a nose. Because the mandalas are a symbol of the unconscious self they also evoke the inward and contemplatory, so that the top areas of both these works contrast with the feet and legs of the lower areas, which are public and active. Although sensuality oozes from these works, they evoke partition, separateness, and then coming together, and the screen becomes the division between the inner, private, and outer, public, self.

Light on water, which sometimes contained the human form, fascinated David Hockney (*b.*1937), and was one of the stimuli underlying his theme of the swimming pool, which has recurred in his paintings since his first visit to Los Angeles in 1964. But such pools were also

Fig.43
Allen Jones
Painted Screen (five panels)
1965
Oil on wood
180 x 211 cm (71 x 83 in)
Private collection
© Allen Jones

Fig.44
Allen Jones
Female and Male Diptych (two panels)
1965
Oil on canvas
183 x 306 cm (72 x 120½ in)
Hirshhorn Museum and Sculpture
Garden, Smithsonian Institute,
Washington D.C.
© Allen Jones

expressions of volume and emptiness as well as solidity and transparency. The way Hockney portrayed their reflecting and refracting surfaces has often been likened to Japanese wood-block prints and Art Nouveau, but it seems likely that his interest in the folding screen was stimulated by an actual visit to Japan in 1971. These interests came together in the famous *Paper Pools* series of 1978, twenty-seven portrayals of a particular swimming pool in different light and weather conditions, during night and day, carried out on colour-infused, hand-made paper. Originally, Hockney intended to mount all twenty-seven of these six foot by seven foot images as three-panel folding screens. Ultimately, only two were, one a portrayal of the pool at midnight. Most of these pools are dominated by the tapering long rectangle of the diving board, which rises from the base of the centre panel up to the middle of the composition, in the daylight pools resembling a pale tapering doorway and at night either a blackened aperture against a luminous building (the underlit pool) or a black bar or phallus overhanging a glowing abyss. In both variants the visual paradox between the solid and hollow shifts back and forth, and if the centre panel of the screen is angled toward the observer and the two outer panels back, this ambiguity is intensified.

If Hockney's pool screens maintain a patterned membrane of implied depth across which the phallic diving board protrudes or appears as a doorway, leaving the observer the apparent option of penetration, then the patterned screens in Henri Matisse's paintings signify the barrier between the observer and the women portrayed. Matisse (1869-1954) has sometimes been criticised as being an excessively decorative painter, but the patterns of the screens in his pictures directly reflect the atmosphere and actions of the seductive women he portrays. Virginia Butera has observed that the unity between the screen and woman (both in the picture are 'decorative') is that the painted screen signifies the sexual act but blocks it, while the painted woman is at once visually accessible yet by definition unreachable.[22]

While Hockney and Matisse saw the screen as a patterned membrane through which the observer might try to pass conceptually, the sculptor Kenneth Armitage (b.1916) has frequently used it as representative of the human torso itself. Originally he made a simple functional screen of corrugated cardboard to hide a stack of his landlady's furniture in his studio in the early 1950s, and the corrugated slab effect became the torsos of his group of three apparently female figures in his *Standing Group* (1952-4). Thereafter, the screen and human torso have interacted, sometimes as one, at other times separated but seemingly in the role of a barrier *vis-à-vis* traveller, hider or seeker.[23] In *The Forest* (1965) arms and legs jut like the limbs of trees from the slab of the screen in which a crowd appears to be crushed in upon itself, and in *Screen, Folded Arms*, a dark grey three-panel screen in painted bronze (the side panels both angled forward), the centre panel is dominated by two thick, menacing, crossed arms. This brooding sculpture gives the impression of something or someone of menace concealed behind

22 Virginia F. Butera, op.cit. p.208.
23 Tamsyn Woollcombe, *Kenneth Armitage: Life and Work*, Lund Humphries Publishers, London 1997.

the screen, or of the screen being visually synonymous with a person being a flowering 'screen' or 'façade' or armoured against what they regard as a hostile world. In *Fleeing Figure* (1977) the human form strives to run through or escape from the panels of the confining screen.

The well-known *Nottingham Screen* (1973), which Armitage made for the library of Nottingham University, is in a different vein: 'an extraordinary form: very economical, and self-supporting because of its zig-zag plan and yet there is no body or "bulk".'[24] Its striding figures represent students and were printed by silk-screen onto its surface; they appear to be walking off the screen, while the long-hatched vertical lines behind reflect the architecture of the university. There could be no greater contrast than between this and the *L-Shaped Screen* (1991) in dark-painted aluminium (fig.45). The rounded, organic shapes of the two people, seated one on each side of the L-shaped partition and joined to it structurally, implying barriers, two figures drawn together yet permanently divided; a persona dependent upon a screen, and a corner of architecture like a house or a wall.

If sexuality and the public and private were the concerns of Pop artists Conner and Jones in their screens, the relationship of landscape and the elements to the mind was the preoccupation of Jim Dine in his *Landscape Screen* (fig.47) of 1969. Dine made a number of versions of this screen, which derived from his earlier painting *Studio Landscape* (1963), and, in a manner typical of the Pop Art format, used obvious symbolism or images in a distorted way to startle the observer. *Studio Landscape*, with its six panels showing darkness, a rainbow, snow falling, grass, yellow sunshine and a blue sky and clouds, all flat, is like six strips of wallpaper juxtaposed with an interior object, a tray with jugs, plates and bottles, still-life elements of the studio, which were attached to the base of a screen panel. There is a 'landscape' with the tools which painted it.

Landscape Screen dispenses with the tray and has five panels: sky, sun, grass, snow and rainbow. Originally this version was silk-screened; the recto and verso of the screen were identical, but the artist painted over the front, intensifying the colour with acrylic, and painted each back panel entirely black, with only the title of the image on the recto of the panel written in white. When the screen folds together, it becomes a unified concept – collective nature – but when opened out each of these aspects of the natural world unfolds and appears as though categorised by the human consciousness which partitions them.

Landscape had concerned the Surrealists. Yves Tanguy (1900-55) had seen Jean Dunand's screens at the 1925 Paris *Exposition Internationale des Arts Decoratifs* and was inspired by them to paint two large four-panel screens, showing two dark, tar-like landscapes under a pink-grey sky with the enigmatic, biomorphic forms which were later so often associated with him. These screens were an extraordinary experiment in space and illusion, for although such open, flat, vast landscapes as

24 ibid.

Fig.45
Kenneth Armitage
L-shaped Screen
1991
Plate and cast aluminium
Height 180 cm (71 in)

Tanguy normally portrayed seem limitless, the darkness of the two screens presses in upon the observer. Other Surrealists who experimented with landscape in the screen include Man Ray, Max Ernst and Salvador Dalí who painted a surreal *trompe l'œil* landscape on a screen constructed by Jean Michael Frank. Man Ray's *Forest* (1950) looms over the observer too, like the claustrophobic jungles of Max Ernst, the 1950 screen having panels which appear to rise like close-ranked tree trunks.

The idea of the screen as an interior/exterior object which relates to landscape and architecture – a partition representing landscape but situated inside the building – is a paradox which found expression in another development, the photographic screen. The American artist Ansel Adams produced a body of landscape screens, making vistas of carefully cropped photographs. These were some of the most important screens to be produced in a period when the folding screen was otherwise in one of its popularity troughs, the 1950s. Adams's screens work because, like a muralist, he knew how to focus upon and isolate crucial parts of the landscape composition in order to enhance the sensation of space, while using the screen's folding nature to stress certain areas of the vista. Certain screens, such as *Clearing Storm*, bear a strong resemblance to Japanese Kano school painting.

The zig-zag nature of the screen was one of its prime attractions for the artists of the 1950s and 1960s. What made the folding screen an increasing concern of fine artists at this time was the failure of interior designers to appreciate it and use it. The desire to take the fine-art painting down from the wall was not in any way unique to the 1960s, but it received greater publicity than before, and the screen offered painters this option.

Leon Polk saw the screen as a natural progression from hanging his large abstract paintings side by side, and in effect, hinging them together, creating all kinds of possibilities by having the abstract colour areas affected by the differing angles. His use of the word 'involvement' in his titles of these screen paintings (titles such as *Two Involvements in One*, or *Seven Involvements in One*, depending on how many panels there were in the screen) reflected this. In the manner of the tea or table screen, he produced a number of table-top folding pictures.

In similar vein, the painter and sculptor Ellsworth Kelly used the screen in an extraordinarily powerful series of paintings in the 1950s, based on sunlight casting broken linear shadows over metal steps. By painting the shadow patterns over nine narrow folding panels based on the steps and then turning the composition side on (as if the stairway was laid sideways on the floor to form a screen) he produced a solid image which appeared to be broken by erratic girder patterns. In 1957 he produced *Seven Sculptured Screens in Brass*, which connects visually with the forty-panel block screens by Eileen Gray. Kelly's work in this area involved abstracting light and shade onto real objects and then reducing these to solid forms which took their structure from the points of junction between the shapes.

Kelly's painting and sculpture is a paradigm of what the screen is to an artist – namely, a form in which space is defined by an acute angle crossing a flat pattern. All screens reduce to this, and are consequently unique among art objects.

Diversity in Form and Function

The last twenty years of the twentieth century have seen the folding screen expand into a wider series of forms than ever before. The rising and falling rhythm of its popularity had taken it to a low point in the 1950s. The 1960s saw it as a vehicle for painting and sculpture but rarely as a credible object of interior design; but in the late 1970s the vanguard of Post-Modernism gave it a vigorous rebirth.

An increased aesthetic tolerance of alternative forms made itself rapidly apparent in interior design in the late 1970s. In Britain this was particularly noticeable in magazines directed at the affluent middle classes, many of whose younger members owned Victorian and Edwardian urban and suburban properties in varying states of repair, and led to a huge renaissance of traditional paint finishes and techniques from rag-rolling and wood graining to murals and *trompe l'œil*.

This generation of young professionals differed from their predecessors in four ways: they were highly eclectic in their tastes, and although affluent lived in very confined spaces, often singly or with a mobile nuclear family. They moved frequently and – especially in Britain during the 1980s – bought property in low-cost areas which they could renovate and sell on. Their properties were often 'listed', with preservation orders on them, and the interior decor which resulted was consequently a renovated period piece in keeping with the house. And increasingly they were single and female, with a more developed interest in decoration than most young single men of equivalent income of previous generations.

The screen fitted into and was often a useful accessory in this lifestyle and decor. The resultant huge variety of designs was probably larger, and the screen probably played more roles, than at any previous time in its history. It became a fine art sculpture; a multi-surfaced or folding painting; a multi-faceted industrial or domestic divider in steel, iron, glass or fibre-glass; a small decorative furnishing; a large practical or decorative object of furniture; a reproduction of any previous period of its existence; or an original design in a traditional style. As a form, the screen had never before served so many purposes.

As a furnishing and decorative art object it remains almost always a labour-intensive, hand-made structure of exclusive design, made largely for the same social groups as it was in previous periods. The large

Fig.46
Reproduction seventeenth-century screen (three panels)
1993
Embossed gilt leather
160 x 140 cm (63 x 55 in)
Courtesy of George Renwick

Fig.47
Jim Dine
Landscape Screen (sky, sun, grass, snow, rainbow) (five panels)
1969
Acrylic on canvas mounted on wood panels
187.3 × 228 cm (73½ × 90 in)
Courtesy of Pace Wildenstein, New York

hotels, private houses, residential and holiday apartments of the upper middle class, for which interior designers constantly work, are the usual places for such screens, and, because of the widespread period decor, approximately forty per cent of them are reproduction screens – that is, close copies in all aspects of a previous design – or of period design, meaning an original design in the style of a particular era.

As before, there is a wide variation in quality and standard. High-quality gilt and leather screens or painted and varnished wooden (usually composition board) three- and four-fold screens in the style of eighteenth-century French and Italian designs, are typical. The painted screens are often finished by distressing – rubbing down the decorated surface with very fine sandpaper to give it an aged appearance – and are then given coats of cracking varnish. This is a complicated process, since the humidity of the air radically affects the behaviour of the varnish. Ironically, this means that more labour goes into producing one of these 'antiqued' screens than generally went into producing their eighteenth- and nineteenth-century predecessors, and if the price of these screens is to accurately reflect the work that has gone into them, it inevitably ensures that they remain exclusive objects.

The problem for the folding screen as a period piece is two-fold. During the later years of the twentieth-century interior design has suffered, as a profession, from a lack of basic technical knowledge amongst many of its practitioners. Pioneer interior designers such as Eileen Gray were technicians and artists par excellence, but many of her successors were not, and as the industry has expanded in the 1980s many have only the sketchiest knowledge of the processes involved in producing the decorative effects and objects which they commission. The result is often a wildly unrealistic expectation of price by the interior designer, which makes the work uneconomic for the supplier. Inevitably, the result of a very low or 'competitive' price is a cheap, inferior object produced by poorly-skilled people, setting a declining standard simply because highly skilled artists cannot afford to undertake time-consuming work for so low a fee. The second problem is that reproduction or traditional design is a cul de sac for creative artists. The work soon degenerates into a mere technical exercise of no conceptual interest.

The domestic decorative screens of the turn of the millennium are mainly commissioned by commercial clients for particular uses and decor. A small central London or New York apartment may have one built to divide a dining area from a sitting room, or a bedroom from a bathroom. Within rooms, smaller screens can be made to hide intrusive pieces of technology which fight with the rest of the decor: small two- or three-panel screens to hide TVs, CD players or computers when not in use. In holiday chalets and cottages which are open to the air they perform the traditional functions of draught exclusion and the shielding of changing and dressing rooms.

This means that the contrasts in style and subject of these decorative objects is enormous. They range from the comic and satirical, such as Val Armstrong's *Jesters* or *Sheherezade* (figs 49, 51) screens, which could fit as easily into a child's playroom as into a drawing room, to Joy de Rohan Chabot's superb *trompe l'œil* screens (figs 52, 53) of casually placed clothes or fabrics, for a hallway or elegant bedroom. Tania Vartan's eighteenth-century chinoiserie is usable in any room with period decor or as a contrast to it (also displaying the much gentler tone of twentieth-century singerie decoration compared to that of the eighteenth), while Sophie Dulud's Art Deco style (fig.59) performs the same function in a room design centred around the 1920s and 1930s.

Trompe l'œil is an outstanding feature of current painted screens, De Rohan Chabot's being typical of folded, draped fabric traditionally associated with the object and its uses, while Charles Hemming's four-panel *Hunting Screen* (fig.55), with its mixture of firearms, hunting equipment, books and trophies, effectively makes the screen a folding wall of shelves, integrating it with the real architecture and furnishings while displaying seemingly tactile illusions. All of these screens are generally constructed of traditional materials, either plywood or composition-board panels or canvas on a wooden frame, and painted sometimes in oil but usually in acrylic because of its rapid drying time. They are normally highly manoeuvrable and of light or moderate weight. It is materials as much as their visual design which segregates the decorative screen from the metal multi-fold and multi-form screens which appear in offices and public buildings as well as in private interiors.

'Fluid space' is the almost literal function of these units. Some, such as the screens of Dyrig Forge, are two panels of woven steel mesh resembling two silver curved pages of a book standing on end, while others, like Habitat's *Boa* screen, resemble a broad short roll of carpet which can be scrolled up when not in use. As display units as much as segregators, made of plywood and mounted on wheels for the exhibition of large-scale graphics, they again take the familiar two- and three-panel format.

Fig.51
Val Armstrong
Scheherazade (three panels)
1996
Acrylic on canvas
165 x 135 cm (65 x 53 in)
© Val Armstrong

Fig.52
Joy de Rohan Chabot
Trompe l'oeil screen
(four panels)
1996
Acrylic on wood
200 x 240 cm
(78½ x 94½ in)
© Joy de Rohan Chabot

Fig.53
Joy de Rohan Chabot
Trompe l'œil screen (four panels)
1996
Acrylic on wood
100 x 210 cm (39½ x 82½ in)
© Joy de Rohan Chabot

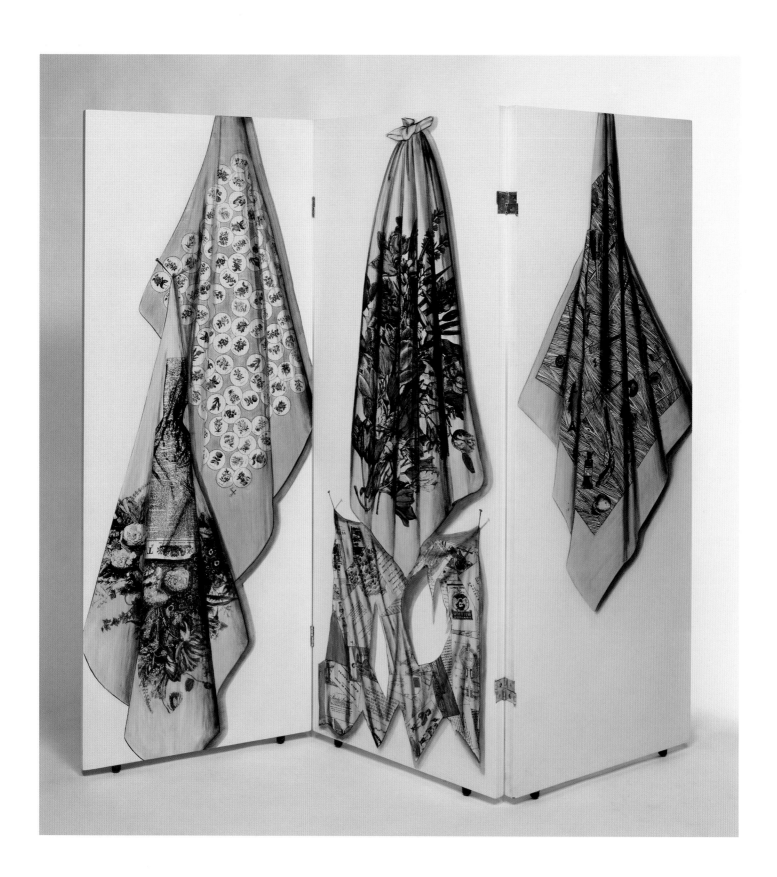

Fig.54
Fornasetti
Scarves (three panels)
1951
Oil on wood
160 x 240 cm (63 x 94½ in)
Courtesy of Imagginazione, Italy

Fig.55
Charles Hemming
Hunting Screen (four panels)
1992
Acrylic on board mounted in
mahoganised frame
190 x 240 cm (75 x 94½ in)
Private collection

Fig.56
Charles Hemming
Monkey Grisaille screen (three panels)
1992
Acrylic on canvas
173 x 122 cm (68 x 48 in)

Fig.57
Charles Hemming
Monkey Grisaille screen (detail)

Fig.58
Charles Hemming
Traveso Screen (three panels)
1996
Acrylic on plywood with antiqued craqueleur finish
180 x 165 cm (71 x 65 in)
Private collection

Fig.59
Sophie Dulud
Art Deco-style three-panel screen
1992
Acrylic on board
175 x 240 cm (69 x 94½ in)
© Sophie Dulud

Fig.60
Frank Beanland
Untitled screen (four panels)
1990s
Oil on canvas on wooden frame
178 x 300 cm (70 x 66 in)
© Frank Beanland

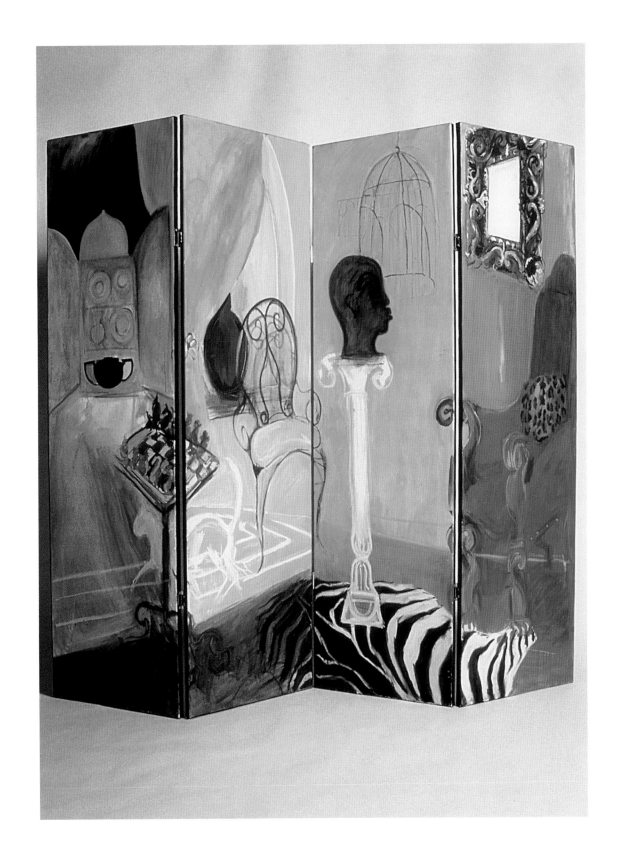

Fig.61
Michaela Gall
Apartment 5a (three panels)
Acrylic on canvas
1990s
152 x 150cm (60 x 59in)
© Michaela Gall

Fig.62
Katy Sayers
Where the Desert Meets the Sea
(five panels)
Oil on canvas
164 x 188 cm (64½ x 74 in)
Private collection

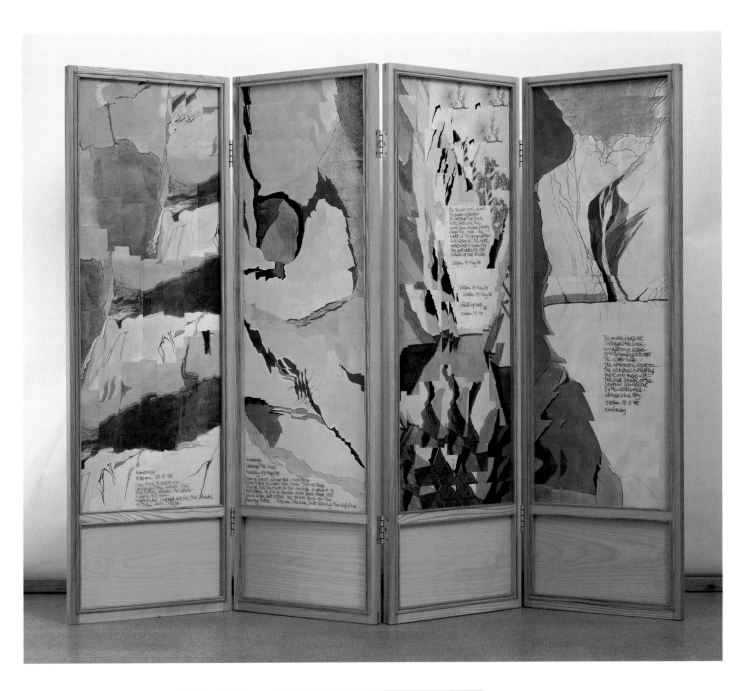

Fig.63
Philip Hughes
Cabbage Tree Creek, Kimberley
(four panels, two sides)
1995
Collage of print on wood
177 x 224 cm (70 x 88 in)
© Philip Hughes
Courtesy of Francis Kyle Gallery

Fig.64
Jerden Krabbé
Borobudur Temple, Java
1992
Oil and gold leaf on canvas
150 x 390 cm (59 x 154 in)
© Jerden Krabbé
Courtesy of Francis Kyle Gallery

Fig.65
Jerden Krabbé
Bandelier Canyon, New Mexico
1992
Oil on canvas
150 x 390 cm (59 x 154 in)
© Jerden Krabbé
Courtesy of Francis Kyle Gallery

Fig.66
Tomoko Azumi
Overture
1997
Steel cabinet with central wood element
and lateral panels in fabric with metal
frame
185 x 52 cm (73 x 20½ in)
© Tomoko Azumi

As commercial furniture, screens have to be elegant, space saving and innovative. Tomoko Azumi's *Overture* (fig.66) is a cabinet with a screen 'wrapped around' it, which, when closed, appears as a circular column enclosing a wooden cabinet, and when opened out becomes two tall, semi-circular sectioned, steel-framed, cotton-covered panels on each side with the cabinet in the centre. These 'form-changers' are exemplified by Capelli's *Ultimate Bookcase*, twelve circular detachable units arranged in three columns of four with rectangular apertures: a screen, a wall, a bookcase and a piece of sculpture.

Some of these are commercially manufactured in number, but the greater number of the most sophisticated designs continue to be built to commission, such as Alex Goacher's square-section steel-frame screens with white, open, makrolon panels, reminiscent of the Vienna Sezession screens; or Andrew Tye's *Eileen*, inspired by the screens of Eileen Gray, forty anodised aluminium panels mounted on eight vertical rods which pivot to create changing spaces.

In the fine works of Andrew Tye (fig.67) and Nina Moeller (figs 68, 69) the borderline between furniture and sculpture blurs. However, Moeller's folded aluminium and kite silk screen adheres more strongly to decorative rather than fine art conventions merely in the decorative use of the silk; it does not assert to be more than a highly satisfying pattern, which is the upper margin of decorative art. The point at which a screen becomes fine art – sculpture or a multi-faceted chromatic work – might be when the practical nature of the structure as a functional object becomes of minimal or no importance compared to the visual appearance and the idea or statement which that visual element seeks to explore or reveal.

This is exemplified in the work of the American Jim Jacobs and the superb 'screens' he produced during the 1980s. These beautiful objects are really free-standing wooden lacquered sculptures, whose connection with the screen is that they have flat vertical surfaces with a recto and verso which are set at angles to one another. The angled panels are reminiscent of the late work of Deskey or Antoni Gaudí, but Jacobs' works do not fold up and their motif cannot be varied. Named after natural features and designed from drawings of them, these include Jacobs' *Marble Canyon*, which imposes (as fine art always does) upon its surroundings and portrays simultaneous series of views or angles of the *Marble Canyon*, becoming a visual descendant of Cubist sculpture.

Jacobs formulated a unique approach to lacquer – drawing in it. By using a quick-drying liquid plastic called Bondo he was able to carve the design with a sculptor's tool, sand the edges of the plastic area flush, and then coat the rest of the screen with chemical-based acrylic and organic nitrocellulose lacquer. It was still a painstaking process, taking up to forty coats, with coloured layers rubbed back to reveal elements of design before being polished with six grades of stones. These sculptural and calligraphic qualities are unique to Jacobs's hybrid screen-

Fig.67
Andrew Tye
S3
1997
Interlinked translucent acrylic: options of
plywood, plastic and wood
186 x 175cm (73 x 69 in)
© Andrew Tye

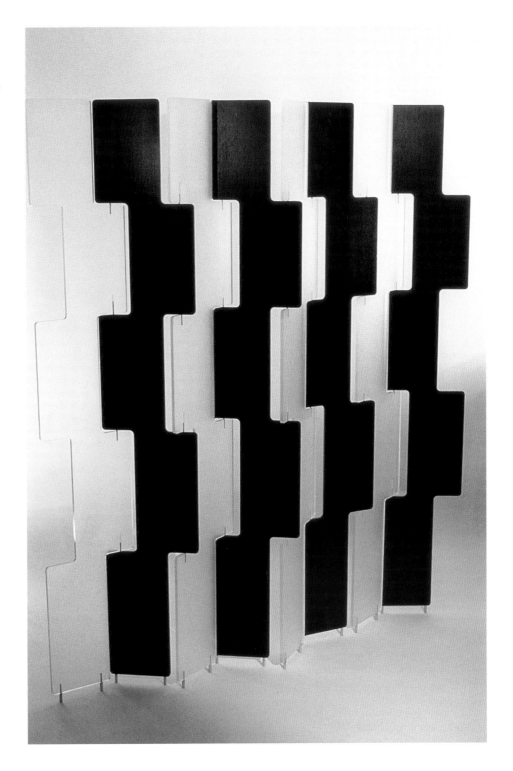

sculptures, and demonstrate not simply a new departure for an ancient
process, but reassert an inevitable gulf which in execution divides the
functional and decorative from the fine art form – the primacy of
concept over function.

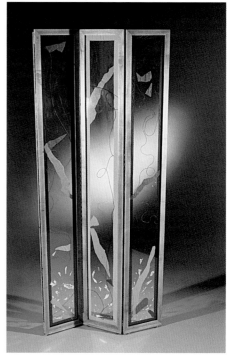

Fig.68
Nina Moeller
Folding screen
1990s
Folded aluminium and coloured kite silk
190 x 120 cm (75 x 47 in)
© Nina Moeller

Fig.69
Nina Moeller
Three-panel screen
1990s
Clear perspex and coloured paper in
American cherry frame
180 x 100 cm (71 x 39½ in)
© Nina Moeller

Fig.70
David Arnold
Screen
1994
Apple and willow twigs painted with flat oil
© David Arnold

Fig.71
Neil Musson
Three-panel screen
1997
American oak frame supporting two layers of
acrylic sheet containing 12v lights
170 x 65 cm (67 x 25½ in)
© Neil Musson

Fig.72
Neil Musson
Three-panel screen
1997
American oak frame with perforated mirrored
acrylic
170 x 195 cm (67 x 77 in)
© Neil Musson

Fig.73
David Graves
Three-panel screen
1990s
Seared sized calico, laced with copper wire
on copper tubing with ebonised ash rails
220 x 128 cm (84 x 51 in)
© David Graves

Fig.74
Charles Eames
Six-panel folding screen
1946
Moulded calico ash plywood and canvas
1036 x 145 cm (408 x 57 in)
© The Museum of Modern Art, New York

The use of glass in screens reaches back through Tiffany and the Pre-Raphaelites to Peter Gambs in the 1830s, but this tradition, too, has been extended if not transcended during the 1980s and 1990s by Patsy Norvell (*b.*1942) and Danny Lane (*b.*1955), both of whom are essentially sculptors.

Norvell's main themes during the early 1980s were transparency, nature and sculpture. At the end of the 1970s she had produced environmental sculpture, including types of fencing, to define and delineate outdoor space, and her first glass screens were amalgams of trellis work, wood and glass panelling reminiscent of the glass-topped French boudoir screens of the 1880s, with the addition of sand-blasted images of flowers and foliage in the glass. The screens might stand inside or out-of-doors. She later dispensed with the wooden frames and hinged fluidly shaped glass panels together, the transparent edges being defined by sand-blasted foliage or left in some cases entirely blank, so that the 'transparent wall' of the screen was in effect dissolving into the air. The loss of the frame and the impossibility of folding the all-glass structures (which were clamped together) moved Norvell's work firmly into the realm of sculpture. Her unfoldable, transparent etched barriers carry the idea of the screen out of the realm of the movable opaque divider into that area of the immovable transparent membrane; a prevention of passage but not perception.

Arriving in the UK in 1975, the American Danny Lane studied stained glass with Patrick Reyntiens and, later, painting with Cecil Collins, while developing applied art objects inspired by Isamu Noguchi. By the early 1980s Lane had discovered what he termed 'painting with light' by cutting, shaping, stacking and sand blasting glass, and rapidly established his reputation for the use of metal and glass or wood and glass simultaneously – materials sometimes thought of as contradictory – in furniture and sculpture.

Lane's glass barriers work as if huge, frosted brush strokes had been drawn in the air, in such pieces as *Mobile Screen*, 1987 (fig.75) and *The Cloud*, 1996 (fig.80). There is great variety in the size and form of Lane's 'screens': some, at around 120 centimetres in height and width, are on a scale common to the traditional folding screen, while others, such as *Wave Wall* (fig.78) at 1600 centimetres in width, are of a size associated with architectural structure. But one of the prime visual elements in Lane's screens is their sense of motion, an element not generally explored in what are traditionally static structures. These pieces do not depend on a motif which depicts movement, as their predecessors might have done, but convey movement in their actual shape and material. Glass is, after all, an exceedingly slow-moving liquid. *Wave Wall* moves, literally, with infinitesimal slowness, while giving the impression of frozen motion; like Norvell's glass screens, it is a physical barrier but a perceptual window into the nature of elemental form.

Fig.75
Danny Lane
Mobile Screen
1987
Twenty-three interlocking pieces of
sand-blasted tempered glass on a
mobile, forged steel drawing
300 x 300 cm (118 x 118 in)
Photograph: Ian McKinnell

At the turn of the millennium Lane's glass screens encapsulate almost all
of the disparate elements and perceptions which have been present in the
different uses and materials of the screen throughout its long history.
The screen is now more varied than ever before, and, like the most
robust of art forms, acquires ever more media for its creation while
retaining and evolving those which it has always employed.

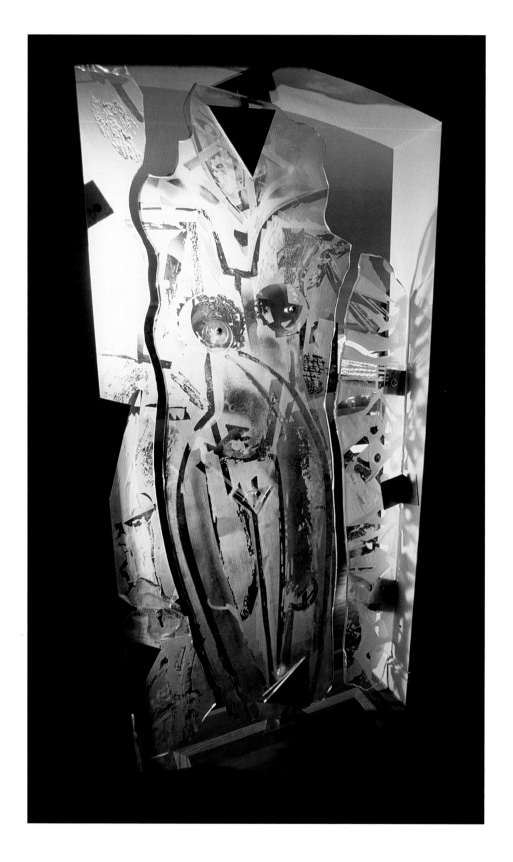

Fig.76
Danny Lane
Pivoting Woman Screen
1987
Sand-blasted glass and steel
220 x 120 cm (86½ x 47 in)
Photograph: Simon Durrant

Fig.77
Danny Lane
Gould's Screen
1987
Sand-blasted and etched glass and steel
120 x 160 cm (47 x 63 in)
Photograph: Klaus Frahm

Fig.78
Danny Lane
Wave Wall
1993
Stacked glass and steel
290 x 1600 x 50 cm (114 x 630 x 19½ in)
Photograph: Julian Cripps

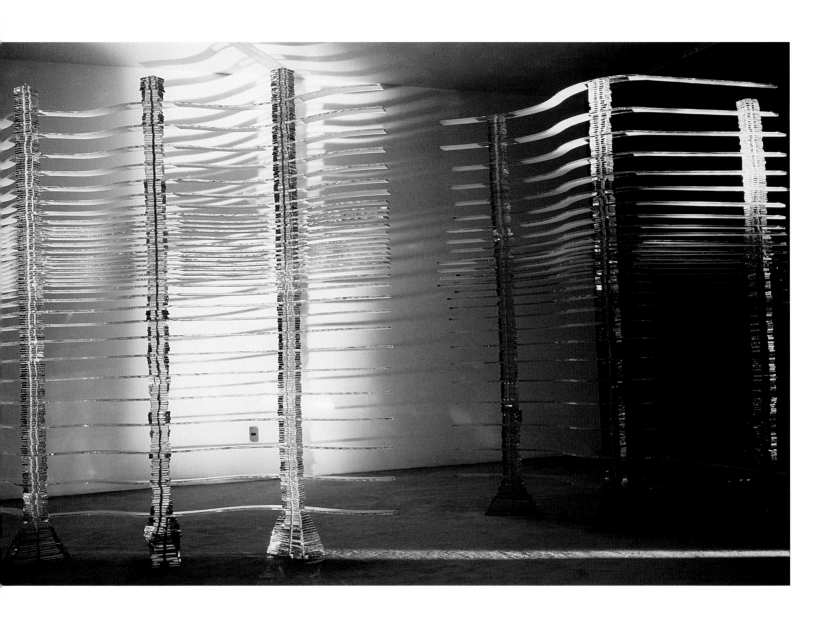

Fig.79
Danny Lane
Wandering Wave
1988
Glass and stainless steel studding
210 x 180 x 50 cm (82½ x 71 x 19½ in)
Photograph: Lorenzo Elbaz

Fig.80
Danny Lane
The Cloud
1996
Sand-blasted glass and steel
(no measurements available)
Photograph: Peter Wood

Fig.81
JAM
3 & 3½ Minutes (three panels)
35 mm movie film and aluminium
Made to order
Photograph: Rob Carter

Glossary

byōbu	the Japanese folding screen.
cartouche	usually an oblong design with rounded corners used as a surround to a decorative pattern.
chinoiserie	Chinese-inspired style, or Chinese objects or decoration.
collage	a decoration made from a variety of materials pasted or attached to a surface.
cornucopia	a horn from which spilled flowers, fruit or riches; a symbol of plenty.
craqueleur	a network of small cracks in a paint surface or varnish, generally from age, or simulated.
dado	a panel covering the lower quarter or third of a wall against which chairs were placed. A corresponding area on a screen for aesthetic purposes.
gesso	a mixture of whiting or chalk with animal-skin glue, forming a paste to create raised details on a design or more commonly applied in thin layers to make an even surface.
gofun	a white, gesso-like substance composed of ground sea-shells.
gouache	opaque water-colours bound with gum.
grisaille	painting in tones of grey, usually to give the effect of sculpture or relief.
Japanning	a European term for any high-gloss lacquered finish.
Kanga	an Edo term for a type of Japanese painting during the Muromachi period based on pictorial styles, subjects and materials imported from China.
lac	lacquer in its raw, grey, resinous form as taken from the *Rhus vernicefera* tree.
putto	(*pl.* putti) a small (naked) boy or angel; a cherub.
recto	the front of a screen, normally the most decorated surface.
shoin	a style of residential architecture for the Japanese élites during the Muromachi period.
tempera	paint made of pigment mixed with egg-white and water when used on paper, or egg-yolk and water when used on gesso or board.
trompe l'œil	a paint technique by which a trick effect of three-dimensionality is produced.
verso	the back of a screen, usually with decoration simpler than that of the front.

Index

Adams, Ansel 104
Aesthetic Movement 78
Alma-Tadema, Sir Laurens 52, 53, 59
Armitage, Kenneth 100-1, *Fig.45*
Armstrong, Val 108, *Figs 48, 49, 50, 51*
Arnold, David *Fig.70*
Art Deco 79, 80, 82, 87, 91
Art Nouveau 32, 33, 68, 69, 73, 74, 76, 100
Arts and Crafts 69
Azumi, Tomoko 124, *Fig.66*

Balla, Giacomo 86, 90
Beanland, Frank *Fig.60*
Beardsley, Aubrey 69
Behrens, Peter 69, *Fig.30*
Bell, Clive and Vanessa 77, 78, 79
Benton, Thomas Hart 68, 87
Blaeu, Willem 40
Bonanni, Filippo 17
Bonnard, Pierre 64, 65
Bonzanigo, Giuseppe Maria 33
Boucher, François 29
Boyd, Muriel 72
Breughel, Pieter the Elder 33
Bugatti, Carlo 72, 74
Burne-Jones, Sir Edward 52

Capelli 124
Carloni, Mario 54
Carlyle, Jane 54
Cézanne, Paul 52, 53, 77, 87
Chanler, Robert Winthrop 76, 77
Chinoiserie 26, 28, 33, 34, 35, 59
Cocteau, Jean 91
Collins, Cecil 132
Conner, Bruce 86, 97, 101
Coromandel 12, 13, 14, 16, 26, 28, 69, 79, 82, 91, *Figs 1, 2*
Corot, Jean 53
Cubism 85, 124

Dadaism 85
Dalí, Salvador 104
Daubigny, Charles 53
David, Jacques-Louis 45
D'Emery, Antoni 17
Degas, Edgar 96
De Lajoue, Jacques 32
Delaunay, Robert 80, 84, 91
Delaunay, Sonia 84
Denis, Maurice 65
De Rohan Chabot, Joy 108, *Figs 52, 53*
Deskey, Donald 77, 82, 84, 85, 86, 91, 124, *Fig.39*
Desportes, Alexandre- François 34, 53
Destailleur, Gabriel Hippolyte 53
De Stijl 85
Dewing, Thomas Wilmer 68, 74
Dijsselhof, Gerrit Willem 73
Dine, Jim 101, *Fig.47*
Duchamp, Marcel 96
Dulud, Sophie 108, *Fig.59*
Dunand, Jean 79, 80, 82, 84, 101, *Fig.36*

Eames, Charles *Fig.74*
Ernst, Max 104

Fornasetti *Fig.54*
Forsyth, James 60
Fragonard, Jean 96
Frank, Jean Michael 84, 104

Fry, Roger 77, 78

Gall, Michaela *Fig.61*
Gambs, Peter 49, 132
Gaudí, Antoni 72, 74, 124
Gauguin, Paul 65, 77, 87
Gebrüder Thonet 73
Goacher, Alex 124
Goncharova, Natalia 91
Gorham Manufacturing Co. 76
Goulden, Jean 80
Grant, Duncan 77, 78, 79, 86, *Fig.35*
Graves, David *Fig.73*
Gray, Eileen 79, 80, 82, 84, 104, 107, 124, *Figs 37, 38*
Greene, Charles 74, 76

Hemming, Charles 108, *Figs 55, 56, 57, 58*
Henley, L.C. 57, *Fig.26*
Hockney, David 89, 92, 93, 97, 100
Hoffmann, Josef 73, *Fig.34*
Hogarth, William 89, *Fig.42*
Hokusai, Katsushika 87
Holland, Henry 45
Hope, Thomas 45
Huet, Christopher 29, 33, 34, 36
Hughes, Philip *Fig.63*

Isokon 80

Jacob, Georges 41
Jacobs, Jim 124
Jacquard 45, *Fig.21*
Jacquemart and Bernard 14, 37, 41
JAM *Fig.81*
Jefferies, Thomas 40
Jones, Allen 97, 101, *Figs 43, 44*
Jouve, Paul 80

Kandinsky, Vassily 87
Kanga 13
Kano school 13, 56, 57, 59, 104
Kelly, Ellsworth 104, 105
Kerr, Eliza 72
King, Jesse Marion 72
Klee, Paul 64-5
Knight, Laura 79
Krabbé, Jerden *Figs 64, 65*

Lancret 29, 32, 33, 52
Lane, Danny 132, 133, *Figs 75, 76, 77, 78, 79, 80*
Larsson, Carl 68, 79
Lebeau, Chris 73
Leleux, Armand 53
Lewis, Wyndham 77
Liberty 56, 69, *Figs 29, 31*
Logan, George 72
Loong, Fow 57

Macbeth, Anna 72
Mackintosh, Charles Rennie 72, 74, 76
McNair, Herbert 72
Maitland, B.F. 72
Man Ray 96, 104
Manet, Edouard 59
Martin, Robert 18
Matisse, Henri 77, 79, 87, 96, 100
Modernism 77, 80, 82, 84
Moeller, Nina 124, *Figs 68, 69*
Mondrian, Piet 85
Monet, Claude 78
Morris & Company 52
Morris, William 52, 53, 65, 76, 77, 80
Mucha, Alphonse 32, 59, 69, *Fig.33*
Musson, Neil *Figs 71, 72*

Nabis 53, 59, 64, 65, 68, 74, 76
Namban 37
Nesfield, William Eden 60, 61
Newman, Carl 87
Noguchi, Isamu 132
Norvell, Patsy 132

Olbrich, Joseph Maria 73
Omega 77, 78, 79
Osawa, Nampo 61

Parker, George 17
Peyrotte, Alexis 34, 35, 45, *Fig.12, 21*
Philpot, Glyn 79, *Fig.41*
Picasso, Pablo 91
Polk, Leon 104
Post-Impressionism 77
Post-Modernism 105
Prendergast, Charles 68, 76, 77
Prendergast, Maurice 77
Pre-Raphaelites 52, 53, 132
Priou, Gaston 84
Pryker, Thorn 73
Pugin, A.N.W. 52

Rateau, Albert *Fig.40*
Redon, Odilon 64, *Fig.28*
Rembrandt, Harmensz van Rijn 57
Renaissance 9, 34, 52
Restoration 45, 89
Réveillon 37, 41
Reyntiens, Patrick 132
Rohlfs, Charles 74
Ruhlmann, Jacques Emile 79
Ruskin, John 52
Russell, Morgan 87
Ryder, Albert Pinkham 68

Sayers, Katy *Fig.62*
Schmied, François-Louis 80
Séguin, Armand 64, 65
Sert, Jose-Maria 91
Shaw, Richard Norman 60
Sheraton, Thomas 45
Shing, Lien 57
Singerie 33, 34, 36
Solomon, Solomon 53
Sougawara 80
Soundbinine, Jean 80
Stalker, John 17
Stevens, Alfred 59
Stickley, Gustave 74, 76
Surrealism 104

Tanguy, Yves 101, 104
Taylor, A.E. 72
Tiffany, Louis Comfort 41, 72, 76, 132
Tosa school 61
Tye, Andrew 82, 124, *Fig.67*

Van de Velde, Henri 72, 73
Van de Rohe, Ludwig Mies 79-80
Van Everen, Jan 86, 87
Van Gogh, Vincent 59
Vartan, Tania 108
Vollmer, Phillip 84
Vuillard, Edouard 59, 64, 65

Watteau, Jean Antoine 29, 32, 96
Whistler, J.A. McNeill 53, 60, 61-2, 64, 68, 87, *Fig.27*
Wingfield, James Digman 57, *Fig.25*
Wright, Stanton MacDonald 87

Yamato-e 12, 13

Zuber and Dufor 37, 45